Dr Neville Staple, 2-Tone Legend, From The Specials..
"Hailing from the same revivalist era as me, The Lambrett
time, still out there performing and entertaining audien
Sanders' book is packed full of photos capturing the nostalgia from a different era
through to the present, telling their story with contributions from the Band, their fans
and some surprises. A must have for everyone's coffee table and my wife Sugary has
ordered extras for supercool gifts!"

Toyah Willcox. Musician, Singer, Actress, Producer, Author…
"Generations to come deserve to experience the youthful rebellion of the Lambrettas
music and Amanda Sanders' book puts it all in context. The musical era between 1978
and the Early 80s was free of media control, a beautiful riot of ideology and passion".

Trevor Laird. English Film & TV Actor…
"It has been my great good fortune over the last 4 decades to have the pleasure of
interacting on many occasions with the Mod community all over the country. The
Lambrettas over that period with their warmth and energy have been great
ambassadors for the modernist lifestyle, and I can't wait to see them on stage again.
Keep up the good work… Trevor Laird – Ferdy in Quadrophenia".

Chris Waddle. Former England Football player, Commentator and Lambrettas fan…
"Hi Amanda. I am really glad that a book is coming out about The Lambrettas. I was
into their music around that time; Poison Ivy was a classic. My favourite song
D-a-a-ance is on my playlist now. It's a credit to the band that they are still gigging
today. Long may it continue…Chris W".

Mike Read. Radio DJ, Broadcaster, Television Presenter…
"How wonderful that there's a book on the Lambrettas. It's always great to have your
achievements documented and it will be a lovely legacy for family, friends and fans as
well as a slice of music history. I'm sure the band will be justifiably proud of having
their own book. I can't wait to read it!
My best, Mike Read"

Dave Davies. Lead Guitarist for The Kinks, Singer and Songwriter…
"In June 1980 my son Martin asked me to take him to the Marquee in London to see
one of his favourite groups The Lambrettas. We went, it was a great show and I thought
they were an exciting band. Good luck with the book! Dave"

David Courtney, Singer-songwriter, Record Producer, CEO / Founder Brighton Music Walk of Fame...

"The Lambrettas played an important part in Brighton's musical history. The band's unique interpretation of Leiber & Stoller's classic song 'Poison Ivy' will stand the test of time. Hats off to my fellow Brightonian Band of Brothers! Wishing great success for the book."

About the author...

Amanda Sanders was born in Eastbourne. She was educated at Micklefield School for Girls in Seaford. Most of her working life was at East Sussex Library Service.. Married to Doug in 1973, they have one son, Ben. She was there from the beginnings of The Lambrettas through to the present day.

BEYOND THE JET AGE: THE STORY OF THE LAMBRETTAS

Amanda Sanders

COUNTRY BOOKS

This book was commissioned by Amanda Sanders
Designed by Dick Richardson
Published by Country Books
Courtyard Cottage, Little Longstone, Bakewell, Derbyshire DE45 1NN
Tel: 01629 640670
e-mail: dickrichardson@country-books.co.uk
www.countrybooks.biz
www.sussexbooks.co.uk

ISBN 978-1-910489-81-9

Dedication

To Doug, we had a laugh, often more in retrospect!
Thank you for taking me along on your ride!
And
To Ben, so you can look back
at what your weird parents got up to over the years!

BACK L-R: *Jim Doyle, Pete Waterman, Peter Haines, David Croker*
FRONT L-R: *Paul, Doug, Sally Atkins, Jez, Mark, Eric Hall*
(See page 17)

CONTENTS

Outside TMC
(See page 31)

INTRODUCTION

I was outside a gig in 2014 with some friends having a cigarette, and we were laughing about some of the weird and wonderful things that had happened to us over the years, when Dave Coombs, said to me "You should write a book". I said I would, and kept meaning to get started, but until now, lockdown 2020, I always used the excuse I was too busy! All of a sudden, I didn't have that excuse anymore!

I decided to put the book together as a light hearted look at the lives and adventures of The Lambrettas over the past 42 years. Although not written as a serious biography, it covers a lot of what happened as it travels chronologically through the years. Some of the stories people sent have been very slightly edited, but they have been left as much as possible in the contributors' own words to keep authenticity, as these are their stories.

I wanted everyone who was in and around the band to have the opportunity to contribute their story. There were some who didn't respond to my request and others who I would have liked to include, but was unable to locate.

It may seem a peculiar decision to write Part 3 in the First Person, so I would like to explain why. It was easy to write Parts 1 & 2 about them, as even though I was there, I wasn't so inextricably linked to everything that was happening because I was at home doing family stuff! However, I was finding it increasingly difficult to continue writing in the same way in Part 3. I kept writing "we" instead of "they", so I gave in to the inevitable.

I'm hoping that I have included enough of the beginnings for the fans from back then to enjoy. I have certainly had a great time taking myself back there over the past few months, and to catch up with some of those people we haven't seen for years. Since 2009 Doug and Paul have said "We know that there are always people who don't embrace change, but hope that people will come and watch us with an open mind and enjoy it for what it is. We have a firm grasp on our heritage, but also a clear idea on the future." I am completely aware that Part 3 covers over ten years of a whole different era, but to write The Lambrettas story without including those years and those people would not be telling the whole story. Since 2009 we've been so lucky and had so much fun, and just as much as catching up with old friends, it has also been great talking to our new friends and including all their contributions.

Amanda Sanders, September 2020

Email: amanda4929@btinternet.com

ACKNOWLEDGEMENTS

My thanks go to ….

Everyone who agreed to send me their memories and pictures to be included in this book. They are: Doug Sanders, Mark Ellis, Paul Wincer, Peter Haines, Sally Atkins, Pete Waterman, Fiona Bird, Jim Doyle, Laura Croker, Derek Haggar, Willie Bourne, Peter Collins, Andrew Gilbert, Ike Nossel, Eddie Piller, Steve James, Patrick Freyne, Dave Purdye, Tim Groves, Paul Macnamara (Mac), Nigel Lavender, Dave Wyburn, Phil Edwards, Jenny Bignell, Rob Wright, Ben Sanders, Cheryl Shaw, Mike Vine, Sean Fletcher, Meurig Jones, Mik & Sue Boon, Dave Walker, Yannic Grangier, Helen Kane, Emily Flood, Nathan Mair, Sandra Pope, Tracey Wilmot, Scott Sunyog, Nick Beetham, Mark Mansell, Steve Goodey, Ant Wellman, David Medland, Richard Anstey, Nicola Eckersall, Eric Hobson, Dan Rehahn, Christine Staple, Tom Fahy, Kevin Crace, Dave Coombs, Stuart Goodwin, Steph Langan, Steve Wilkinson, Chris Pope, Dave Cairns, Mackenzie Gordon-Smith, Guy Denning, Ian Taylor, Gary Shail, Mick Yates, Sara Farah, Alan C. May, Gary Davies & Alison James, Dan Turner, Jay P. Fuller, Tony Boden, Spencer Mumford, Barry Pulfer

Also, to Pete Hammond who agreed for me to take the extract about The Lambrettas from his book, "Get Down Here Quick and Mix Yourself a Hit: Mixmaster, my story".

Dave Coombs who allowed me to use some of his photographs from 2012 to date and Stuart Goodwin who allowed me to use some of his photographs from 2011 to date.

Other photo permissions are: Eric Hobson for Lechlade Festival, Gary Beaumont at www.radiomix106.com for Sabinillas, Harrisonaphotos for Riverside Festival, Pete Connor at Skamouth Official for Lambrettas on stage, David Street at Skamouth Official for mixed artist photo, Sally Newhouse for Great British Alternative Festival, Butlins, Skegness, Fiona Bird for Lewes Bonfire, Rhona Murphy Photography for Novatones on stage, and the Charlie & Shirley Watts PHOTOGRAPH BY GERED MANKOWITZ © BOWSTIR Ltd. 2020/mankowitz.com. Publicity photos for Rocket Records shot by Adrian Boot.

Richard Weaving and the Law family for telling me about Ryan's story, and allowing me to share it.

John Harold and Dawn; for driving down to us so I could take photos of your Cortina Mk 2.

Doug, Ben & Emily thank you for the past 3 months. You have all patiently listened to my musings; I saw the raised eyebrows and looks of resignation when I said for the hundredth time; "Can I just ask what you think of this?" You still gave me your time over and over. Emily for those many hours of proof-reading. Doug for cooking, cleaning and cups of tea. I love you all xxx

Finally thank-you to Phil Johnson for his perfect advice and cover design; and to Dick Richardson of Country Books for giving me the confidence to believe I could do it. He transformed my words and hundreds of photos into a real book, and he guided me through every process with such kindness and patience.

PART ONE 1979-1982

Doug Sanders started learning to play the guitar in his early teens, along with some classmates; all playing various instruments and all having a passion for music. He went to Priory School in Lewes, which, during the era he was there, produced what seemed to be more than their fair share of Artists and members of Bands. Among these are: Elvis Costello's Attractions, Wreckless Eric, M., Scritti Politti, The Lambrettas, The Piranhas and The Pogues.

Doug: When I was 14, I went to the 1969 National Jazz and Blues Festival held on Plumpton Racecourse, 5 miles outside Lewes. I got talking to a guy about learning the guitar and said I was getting on well. The guy said "How many chords do you know?" I replied "How many are there?" When he told me there were thousands, I remember thinking Oh shit! I thought I was mastering it! Over the festival the guy showed me quite a few chords on his acoustic, and after the initial shock of realising I had a lot more to learn, I just got down to it, and have spent most of my time ever since playing.

As soon as he was able, Doug started playing in local bands around his home town of Lewes. In

National Jazz & Blues Festival, Plumpton

Doug with Oakenlode at Watchfield Festival, 1975

Songwriting at Doug's house

the 1970's he was in bands called Oakenlode and then Shakedown. There were various incarnations of Shakedown, all of which included Doug, and around mid-1978 he got new kid around town, Jez Bird to join them. Doug and Jez were into the same kind of music and agreed they were looking for a different direction than the others, so decided they would move on and start something new. Both could sing and play guitar, so they set about to write some new songs. On 15th January 1979 they got together at Doug's house to start this new project.

Shakedown

Doug: I was sitting at my dining room table in 1979 writing a song with Jez called 'Runaround'. My wife Amanda came in and said *"You two should write a song called Beat Boys in the Jet Age"*. She'd seen it in a book she was reading...so that's exactly what we did. We decided it was a good title track, so if you don't like it, or even if you do, blame Amanda!

While Doug and Jez were writing their new songs, they still played gigs with Shakedown until their replacements were found. By March they felt they were ready to get some other members to join them. They saw an ad in a music shop in Brighton from a bass player looking for a band, so they rang the number.

Mark Ellis: Early 1979. I had been back in England a few months; living in a crappy bedsit. No phone. I had an ad up in the local music shop in Brighton. A friend of mine's number was used in the ad. The responses I'd got from musicians were not promising, so I was thinking of returning to the U.S. My mate told me he'd had another call, and I decided I wouldn't bother replying. But he said something sounded good about it. So, I called, spoke to Doug, and it did sound interesting. After talking to Doug, we made arrangements to get together. He met me at Lewes station. I remember carrying my bass, as I was walking with him to his home, talking about music. We sat in a room and tried a few songs. I thought it was going well, and hoped he did. Doorbell rang, Jez arrived. Then the three of us played for a while. I don't recall if they told me that night I was 'in' – but I heard later Doug had given the "thumbs up" to Jez when he met him at the door. We started looking for a drummer. Auditioned a few, but no luck. Then we heard about Paul from Doug's mum. He was friends with someone she worked with. There was no wondering if Paul knew about the Mod revival. In he walked, parka, suit, all the gear. And ready to drum. So, we nabbed him. And now the band was complete.

Paul Wincer: I got a call one evening from Doug Sanders. He said I've been recommended to call you as I hear you are a drummer, and by all accounts not bad. Doug's mum was working with a school friend of mine, Leigh Croucher, and he had said to give me a call. "*We've got a band going and we're into this Mod thing*", he said. I replied, quite excited, saying I am too and I'm probably the only mod in Seaford. It was decided that I should try out for the band in Lewes. I couldn't drive then, so Jez came over to

Jez's morris minor van

collect me in his morris minor van. He arrived wearing a parachutist type jumpsuit, which didn't strike me as particularly mod, but never mind I thought. So, we arrived and I set up my drums and we were off. It all went very well. I was enlisted there and then and was rewarded with a Lambrettas sticker planted on my forehead!

Over the next few weeks, Doug, Jez, Mark and Paul rehearsed as much as they could, learning all the new songs that Doug and Jez had written, along with some others that they all wrote together. They were planning to be out gigging by mid-June and started booking themselves around Brighton. They needed to choose a name, and at this time, although the "mod revival movement" had been growing since 1978, it was still not mainstream, so they decided to make it obvious what they were about! Doug has always explained it as follows: *"There were only a few Mods locally in Brighton and Hastings and we had no idea there would be a revival on the scale that it grew into. That's when we decided to call the band The Lambrettas to make it as obvious as possible, so that people would know what we were about."*

Lewes Mods

The Lambrettas were getting themselves ready for gigging. They had the name and the songs and had managed to get most of their stage clothes from charity shops, although Doug was lucky enough to be given a suit from Charlie Watts of the Rolling Stones! Doug's dad (Doddie) was friends with Charlie and his wife Shirley when they lived in

Lewes. Doddie was a jockey back in the 1950's and 1960's and was proficient in the art of mane pulling. He did this for Shirley's horses, and they used to sit in the kitchen and put the world to rights. Charlie gave Doddie the suit and also a psychedelic shirt that was Mick Jagger's, which Doug still occasionally wears on stage now.

LEFT: *Mick Jagger's shirt 1982*

ABOVE: *Mick Jagger's shirt 2015*

RIGHT: *Pass for Newmarket*

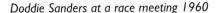

Doddie Sanders at a race meeting 1960

Charlie & Shirley Watts in Lewes

Mark: When I was younger, the first celebrity I had ever seen and met was Charlie Watts from the Stones. I always remember he had on an immaculate cream-colored suit. Years later, not long after The Lambs formed, Doug showed up looking very sharp. He had on the very same suit that had belonged to Watts. Charlie had given it to Doug's dad, I believe.

At one of the Scout Hut rehearsals a friend of Mark's came down on his scooter with a camera. So, they thought they would have a go at taking some photos. These were the first ones taken of them as a band, and Doug is wearing Charlie's suit.

First group photos at the Scout Hut

Beat Boys stickers

Amanda: We got some sheets of stickers printed which just said The Lambrettas Beat Boys in the Jet Age. Before they had even done a gig, Me, Doug, Jez, and a couple more friends went up to London for the day! We just spent the whole day travelling the underground, and we all had sheets of the stickers which we stuck on all the advertising boards up the escalators. There was no CCTV then and we knew it would be the best bit of self-promotion we could do. Even though people at that time wouldn't know what it meant, later when The Lambrettas were mentioned, they would go "I've heard of them, not sure where from though!" We never really knew if our idea worked, but it was a great day!

Doug: In June 1979 we were ready to get out and play some gigs. We had some booked in Brighton and Lewes, but then we found out that Chicane had pulled out of a Mod-Day on Hastings Pier. We managed to get hold of the guy who was putting on the event, Peter Haines, and blagged a short set from him. So, 9th June 1979 was our first gig and we set off to Hastings Pier taking the usual suspects of our mod friends with us to support us. Once there, they split into small groups and dispersed through the audience talking loudly about us, saying *"The Lambrettas are on today, I've heard they're a great band!"* It worked, and after a while they could hear other people saying the same! Of course, they also had the famous stickers which were duly stuck everywhere around Hastings. We were all really nervous as it was the first gig, but we were fine once we were on stage. Afterwards, we agreed a management deal with Peter Haines which took us to Rocket Records and beyond.

Mark, Jez and Wilbo on Hasting Pier

Doug, Amanda and Mods, Hastings

Peter Haines: I decided to sign The Lambrettas after that Hastings Pier gig because I actually thought they were the best band on the bill! I remember Doug hassled me a lot at the gig, which I liked. Ultimately, I was a willing victim, as I could see the whole band were committed. Also, as anyone could see, Doug is a great person and I knew I could work with him.

Things started to move really quickly after the Hastings gig. They signed a management deal with Peter Haines, and he was contacted by an A&R person from Rocket Records, Sally Atkins. Rocket had been advertising in the music press for bands to make a new album. '*We are a young successful name record company and we want to record the sound of today and get it out next week. If you think your bands got that sound, ring 499 2139 now*'. Hundreds sent in demo tapes, and 12 bands were chosen. Although The Lambrettas had not seen the advert and did not ring the number, Sally had heard about them, and they were added just in time to the album. The songs for all the bands were recorded at Pathway Studios with Pete Waterman who at the time worked for Rocket, working with the bands to do some production on their songs. They signed a contract with Rocket for their song on 31st August 1979. Once the album was released, one track from one band was to be chosen as a single, and this ended up being 'Go Steady' by The Lambrettas.

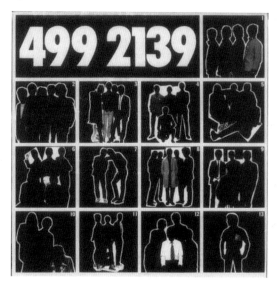 

499 2139 cover

Peter Haines: I remember that for some reason Doug and I were up in London, just the two of us. We were waiting for a meeting, sitting in a corridor. It was either an agent or a record or publishing company. We were trying to blag a deal, obviously before

Rocket came on the scene. Along came Steve Lewis from Virgin Records who was also visiting. So, we three were talking and Doug said "*Bring out the Branson*". I cringed a bit but Steve Lewis thought it was hilarious!

Sally Atkins: I was a new young Head of A&R at Rocket Records, so my boss suggested I work with a more experienced consultant, enter Pete Waterman. I had recently failed to sign Madness to the label despite being in the chase when they first appeared on the scene. They didn't consider Rocket a very cool label and wanted to sign to a more maverick label like Stiff Records which of course they did with huge success. Pete and I were looking at ways of attracting the best new talent and he had the inspired idea of placing an anonymous ad in the NME, looking for new bands for a compilation album.

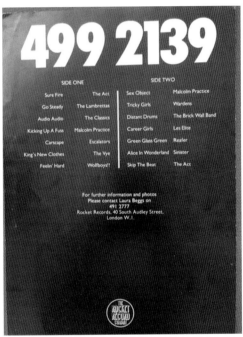

Pete Waterman: I was pretty busy at the time. I'd been working with The Specials and then I went to work at Rocket as a consultant. I liked David Croker, who was the MD of Rocket Records at that time, and I wanted to work with him. He asked me to work on some concepts with Sally Atkins to get some acts for Rocket. I came up with the phone number idea just to raise awareness, but I wanted it to be sorted quickly. "*Come into the studio, record your song and bugger off*".

I liked The Lambrettas as well, they were a bit cooler than most of the bands, and they understood where the market was and wanted more out of it. When I saw them, they were the obvious choice! We recorded 'Go Steady' as their song for the album. I said to David Croker, we should do this band.

Amidst all the things going on with Rocket Records, The Lambrettas were playing around Brighton and smaller London gigs, and were getting quite a good following. Their 15th gig was booked for 22nd September 1979 at the legendary Marquee Club in Wardour Street. They were all pretty confident at their gigs in Brighton as it was home territory, but weren't sure how many would turn up to The Marquee, so Amanda and Fiona (Jez's then girlfriend, who later became his wife) organised a coach to go from Lewes to the gig.

There were some friends of The Lambrettas from Lewes who were always around and went with them to just about everything they did at the beginning, and they need a mention. There was John Gosling & Lav (Ian Lavender); Martin R, Crow, Shelley, Wilbo, Martin H and Gavin. They went to the first Hastings Pier gig, all the Brighton gigs, The Marquee, on the back of the lorry, down the scout hut, and round Doug and Amanda's house all the time.

Doug and Amanda's House

Fiona: We made tickets for the Marquee from library cards which we typed the info onto, and sold them for £2.25 each; this covered the coach hire and entry to the Marquee. We thought if we took 50 people with us who were ready made fans, it would help to make the gig look a bit fuller! Rocket Records were coming and we wanted to impress them so they chose The Lambrettas for the single deal from 499 2139!

Doug: When I'm asked about my most vivid memory, I always remember that first Marquee gig. We had travelled up in our van, and Amanda and Fiona brought a coach from Lewes. Once the Lewes and Brighton people were in there it still looked empty and we were back in the dressing room when they told us that the doors were about to open. I went and looked outside the door and there was a queue all the way up Wardour Street. It was such a buzz! When we went out there it was so hot, a great atmosphere, and each time the crowd moved forward, so did a heat surge. I realised at that point, this has finally gone beyond the pub gig band, which was what I'd always hoped for. There are so many elements as to how a band might climb a rung of the ladder: time, place, luck and some music stuff. I think at the beginning what we lacked in experience and finesse, we made up for in energy and enthusiasm. It's tough out there, as anyone in a band will tell you, always has been. How many rungs can you climb? Will you fall off? One thing's for sure, there is no formula. Strangely, 40 years on, a TV auction programme had some lining boards from the dressing room of The Marquee, which my son noticed by chance. It says "LAMBOS", and I can see it's my writing.

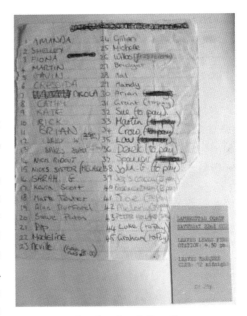

Marquee Coach ticket & list of passengers

LAMBOS on Marquee Dressing Room lining boards

Mark: The first time we played the Marquee, we hired a bus to bring friends, fans and family along to the gig in London. It was a fantastic night. Incredible to think of the legendary names who played on that stage, and here we were.

Rocket Records had organised for a photographer to be at The Marquee gig, and some of these photos were subsequently used for the cover of the single 'Go Steady'.

Amanda: The coach trip was so much fun. Everyone had such a great evening, at the gig and also on the coach, that when we got back to Lewes quite a few people didn't want to go home, so they all came and stayed at our house. I can remember making so many fried egg sandwiches for people at 3am, and then Doug and the band arrived back and we just stayed up all night as we were all buzzing from the excitement. We knew Rocket were going to choose The Lambrettas for the single deal!

People from Marquee coach

After the Marquee gig, they started to get bookings further afield, but for a few months they still had their day jobs. Paul worked in a furniture showroom, Mark wasn't working at the time, Doug was a milkman in Lewes and Jez was a baggage handler at Gatwick Airport. They would often collect Jez from Gatwick on the way to a gig, and drop Doug at the Milk Depot on the way home. They were both so exhausted that they decided to take a chance and left their jobs at the end of October 1979 in the hopes they could make enough money to live being musicians.

Go Steady was released as a single on 9th November 1979. Quite quickly it got into the bottom end of the UK single charts.

Go Steady cover

On the middle black part of the vinyl, between the end of the groove and the label is where the barcode is usually scratched on before pressing, so it is reproduced on every record. On 'Go Steady', Jez also scratched *'Yes she's really going out with him'*, and on the B side *'Beat Boys of the '70s'*. Jez's wife, Fiona has agreed to this being included in the book. It was a personal message to her from Jez as they had only recently started going out, and "their song" was the Joe Jackson hit 'Is she really going out with him'.

Amanda: One or two people have told us that they are pictured on the cover of 'Go Steady', but the most emotive story I heard was quite recently; In 2018 I received an email from someone called Richard, who was after some autographs from the band for his wife, her sister and their mother. Richard said *"In the top front picture, the guy in the grey suit in between Doug and Jez, with a pint in his hand, was my father in law, Ryan Law. He sadly passed away from a rare and progressive form of Alzheimer's disease in October 2018 at the age of 54. He was an avid fan of The Lambrettas, and very active on the MOD scene, and one of his proudest moments was being pictured on the Go Steady cover."* Ryan would have been 15 when photographed at The Marquee. Doug, Paul and Mark signed three record sleeves and we sent them to Richard along with some other things, which Richard gave to Ryan's wife Sally and daughters Grace and Emily for Christmas in 2019. As we also lost someone too soon, it just reminds one how precious life is and how we all have to grab everything that comes along and enjoy every moment.

Paul: One idea Rocket Records had to promote 'Go Steady', was to hire a large flatbed truck and driver, complete with a generator on the back. They then arranged for us to go to 4 different towns around Sussex and to play Go Steady with a couple of other songs, parking up close to pre-agreed record shops in the centres of each of the towns. It was advertised during the previous week in the record shops. We took quite a few of our friends along with us in a few cars that Sally Atkins and others from Rocket were driving round behind the lorry. Obviously as soon as the lorry stopped, they all climbed up on the back to dance and sing along. First was Haywards Heath, then Lewes, then Brighton and finally Worthing. We attracted big crowds in

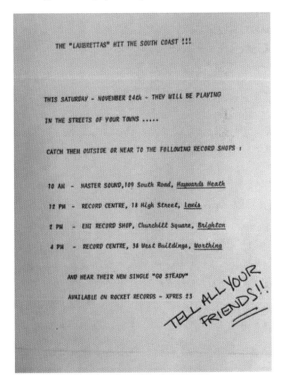

THE "LAMBRETTAS" HIT THE SOUTH COAST !!!

THIS SATURDAY - NOVEMBER 14th - THEY WILL BE PLAYING

IN THE STREETS OF YOUR TOWNS .....

CATCH THEM OUTSIDE OR NEAR TO THE FOLLOWING RECORD SHOPS :

10 AM - MASTER SOUND, 109 South Road, Haywards Heath

12 PM - RECORD CENTRE, 18 High Street, Lewes

2 PM - EMI RECORD SHOP, Churchill Square, Brighton

4 PM - RECORD CENTRE, 38 West Buildings, Worthing

AND HEAR THEIR NEW SINGLE "GO STEADY"

AVAILABLE ON ROCKET RECORDS - XPRES 13

TELL ALL YOUR FRIENDS!!

all the towns as it was such an unusual thing to see along with the Saturday shoppers. There were people waiting at all the record shops, and then they followed the lorry around. In Haywards Heath and Lewes, we had a police escort out of town, but we got to play and they didn't bother us too much. It was slightly more

Lorry at Lewes Record Centre

difficult in Brighton as we gridlocked Churchill Square right in the centre, but for the most part they let it slide and were just glad to see the back of us. However, the Worthing constabulary had heard we were on the way and weren't quite as friendly. It was the shortest of the stints before we were run out of town.

Sally Atkins: A Pete Waterman idea…he wanted to cause a publicity stir; he was thinking of the Beatles playing on the roof of the Apple building. Our slightly more modest plan was to disrupt Brighton by having the band play live on the back of a flat-bed lorry. We did cause some traffic jams, I can't remember how much publicity we created but I do know I had never heard of a risk assessment at the time and in retrospect, am just relieved that none of the band fell off the back of the lorry when it was driving along!

On 20th November 1979, just after 'Go Steady' was released, the band signed a three-year record deal with Rocket Records. This was backstage at The Nashville in Kensington where The Lambrettas were playing with two of the other bands from 499 2139; The Act and Malcolm Practice. They were looked after pretty well by Peter Haines at this time, and he spent a lot of time fighting their corner for them. He used to personally deliver demos to record companies and event info to music papers so they didn't get lost, or more likely, ignored, and he just generally created a buzz with the agents who used to talk to record companies.

THE
NASH VILLE
ROOM
Twist and Twang with Rocket
on Tuesday, Nov. 20th
(adm. £1)
THE LAMBRETTAS **THE ACT**
MALCOLM PRACTICE
Artists from the new album
'499 2139'

Peter Haines: I worked pretty hard to get those London gigs, and always made sure they were in the music paper listings. I networked a lot at that time and was always pestering record companies to come along to gigs. Living in Hammersmith was crucial and I knew everyone at the Marquee Club where I hung out a lot. I was friends with Simon Fuller and he was very much part of the scene, as he was manager of The Teenbeats, who I managed before The Lambrettas. Huggy Leaver was my best friend at Hastings college. It was great to sign a proper deal for my band. I decided that although Rocket was a small team, it ensured we didn't suffer loss of dedication and enthusiasm as we might have done at the hand of a major like CBS.

They were always visiting Rocket's offices at Lancaster Gate, and as Peter says, because they were a smaller team, there was always someone they knew who would be around. The people they seemed to deal with most were David Croker who was MD, John Hall, Head of Promotion, who later became MD when David left. Head of A&R was Sally Atkins, Laura Croker (née Beggs) was the Press Officer, Helen Dann – PA to John Reid, and Robert Key was International Manager. In publishing were Eric Hall and his assistant Jim Doyle. Jim took over after Eric left. (*Prelims page VI for picture.*)

Amanda: I have Helen Dann to thank for putting me in touch with a few of the above so I was able to add their stories.

Jim Doyle: The thing I remember most is what a great bunch the members of the band were and how their different personalities seemed to work so well when they performed. They really enjoyed the success, but kept their feet on the ground. They had an array of stories which kept us fully entertained whenever they came into the office. It's a shame that I do not recollect any of their actual stories.

Laura Croker: I was Press Officer at Rocket Records during the time The Lambrettas were on the label, and I oversaw their publicity. It was always fun being around them and hearing all their Brighton stories.

Sally Atkins: The first time I came to Sussex to meet the band. I had the address (for Doug and Amanda's house) but wasn't sure how to find it so, on reaching Lewes, I stopped in my company car (a bright orange mini!) and asked for directions. Whoever it was that I asked, their response was "Oh you'll be from Rocket Records, looking for Doug Sanders". Small towns!

The band had been so busy through December and January, they decided they needed a bit of help with driving and equipment, but wanted someone they knew and trusted. Derek Haggar started driving them up to Tooting Music Centre where they were recording songs for singles and their first album. He had done some Roadie things with Doug and Jez in previous bands, and was with them where ever they went after this, so was really like a fifth Lambretta for a couple of years.

On 8th January 1980 they did their first TV appearance on a Granada show called Get it Together. They played 'Go Steady' and 'Listen Listen Listen'.

> **Doug**: It was our first TV appearance; it was live and was a bit of a baptism of fire! There were 'men in white coats' doing the sound, and it wasn't great…but it was nevertheless a TV show!

Although he had been driving them to TMC, the first gig Derek drove them to as a Roadie was on 2nd February 1980 at The Norbreck Castle in Blackpool.

> **Derek**: The very first gig I took them to was a massively long drive. The band van was an old twin wheel base ex-ambulance. We were friends, but I know they all picked me to be their Roadie because I was good at repairing vehicles; even though I was actually an aircraft mechanic, it was close enough for them. In fact, on the way back from that gig in Blackpool, I had to repair a wheel that Jez had wrongly fixed! We used to pile in the van like you wouldn't do these days, and make seats with the gear in the back for people to sit on! After driving most of the night, the first person we dropped off that early morning was Fiona. She always faffed around, and she was taking ages saying goodbye to Jez. From the back of the van Doug piped up, "*Oh come on, it'd be nice to get home before the MOT runs out!*"

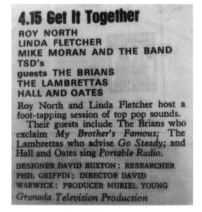

TV Listing

Jez trying to fix the van

On 14th February The Lambrettas released their second single, 'Poison Ivy'. There was a lot of criticism at the time of the 'Two Stroke' label that it was released under. Rocket Records were convinced it was a good bit of publicity, and thought it was funny, but the band members were incredibly embarrassed as they thought it was in bad taste. They knew they would get some criticism and it would damage their pretty fragile credibility with the music press. However, Rocket won the argument and they went ahead with the Two Stroke label and image on the cover. Urban myth says that they had to withdraw this label as they were threatened with legal action, and re-press on the Rocket Label, and that Rocket had done this to make fun of Two Tone. This wasn't true, Rocket were not making fun, they just thought it was a funny joke, and so the first 5,000 were pressed this way, the rest, as always intended, were pressed with the Rocket Label.

> **Sally Atkins**: When we released Poison Ivy, someone, probably Pete, had the brilliant idea of releasing it on a label called Two-Stroke, with artwork echoing Chrysalis Records Two-Tone label.

Doug has always said "*Poison Ivy It's a blessing and a curse!*"

> **Doug**: We obviously have to play 'Poison Ivy' at gigs, which I don't mind. Particularly more so in recent times as we have a permanent brass section, so this helps and it sounds pretty good, although it is fair to say that it is not very representative of the rest of our songs. Having said that, it doesn't have any effect one way or the other nowadays, but when we first started it was probably misleading for some people.

Peter Collins produced 'Poison Ivy', along with all the songs from their first album 'Beat Boys in the Jet Age'. At the time Peter Collins was a business partner of Pete Waterman, they had a production company called 'Loose Ends'. Pete Waterman was the person who suggested the second single should be a cover, and came up with 'Poison Ivy' as an idea.

> **Pete Waterman**: I was working with Peter Collins when we were thinking of The Lambrettas next single. I had worked with a band in the '60s called The Mighty Avengers. They were a great live band and they played 'Poison Ivy', and I always liked it. I said to Peter Collins "*This song Poison Ivy is a hit, always has been a hit*". So, we recorded it.
>   I remember I got Peter Collins to come and watch The Lambrettas early on at a club in Birmingham, and I met him at the railway station and we went to the gig. It was the day after their first appearance on Top of The Pops. Peter had bought 2 cigars which we smoked that evening – we thought "**We've cracked it!**"

Paul: We were running through 'Poison Ivy' in the studio and it was all sounding good. Pete Waterman had suggested trying it out as a cover. Peter Collins suggested adding in brass and Waterman said, "*Right let's try some brass on this then*". I said "*You what? It'll sound rubbish!*" He replied with "*Right you, out of the studio and come back in a few hours*". So, I went to the pub, mumbling under my breath about how soft and pansy it was all going to sound. The others stayed behind. On my return he says, "*Right then, listen and don't say a word*". I think I had to eat a huge chunk of humble pie on that one, and had to admit it sounded brilliant. Maybe that was why they were producing and not me. I still to this day don't know where the cowbell count in came from. It was something I just did with no prompting, and it stuck.

Doug: At first, we weren't sure, we were in no way coerced and could have gone down a different path, but we ran through it a few times to get the arrangement. The song had been done many times; The Coasters, Rolling Stones, etc., but all were the same style and tempo. After a bit I tried a 'chop offbeat rhythm'. It just made it a lot more dancy! It did lean towards the ska thing, but it wasn't planned to be like that. Peter Collins had the idea of the brass charts which also worked really well. He got in 3 great session players, and I soon discovered one of them had played with John Mayall's Bluesbreakers, which I thought was really cool!

'Poison Ivy' got to number 7 in the UK music charts, and the band received a silver disc for sales of over 250,000. These were Pete Waterman's and Peter Collin's first silver discs. Mike Stoller was in the UK in 1980 and Rocket arranged for The Lambrettas to meet him.

1980 was a whirlwind of gigs, recording and TV appearances for The Lambrettas! Their first appearance on Top Of The Pops aired on 6th March 1980 playing Poison Ivy. TOTPs was always recorded the day before.

L-R: Paul, Mark, Mike Stoller, Doug, Jez

Doug: It's strange how things get ticked off an 'I would like to do/be list'. Initially I remember watching local bands aged about 13/14 and thinking *"One day I might make it to there"*. TOTPs was a dream I thought at that time to be way out of my reach! Then there we were at the studios doing just that. And here I was on 5th March 1980 standing outside the studio door, but still in the BBC building sharing a Number 6 with Dave Wakeling from The Beat.

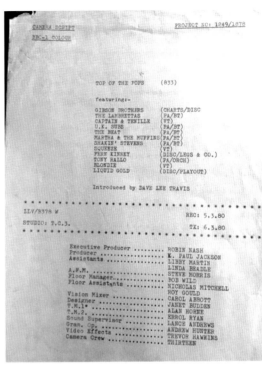

Mark: First time we got to do Top of the Pops – what an amazing feeling. I'd been watching that show most of my life, and now I was appearing on it. And less than a year after The Lambs had formed.

Derek: That first Top of The Pops, we were there with The Beat, among others. It was time for them to be on stage in the studio to do their performance of 'Hands off She's Mine', but they couldn't find Saxa. There was a bit of a panic as time schedules have to be kept to as much as possible at the BBC! He was eventually found in a room with a bottle of vodka, and off he went to the stage and of course the performance was fine, being they were only miming obviously.

During March and April 1980, they played 'Poison Ivy' on quite a few TV shows. Two more times on TOTPs, which aired on 20th March and 3rd April. Tiswas on 22nd March and Cheggars Plays Pop on 14th April

Join in the fun with The Lambrettas and Barbara Dickson, who are among Keith Chegwin's special guests in today's Cheggers Plays Pop 4.20 pm

4.20
Cheggers Plays Pop
starring **Keith Chegwin**
with special guests
The Lambrettas, Barbara Dickson
and **Pussyfoot**
this week's hit sounds and top pop fun and games. The irrepressible Cheggers will be assisted by VIVIENNE MCKONE and GORDON ASTLEY leading their twin teams the 'Yellows' and the 'Reds'.

Designer BARRY ROACH
Director JOHNNIE STEWART
Producer MIKE STEPHENS. BBC Manchester

Radio Times

Doug: When we were No. 7 in the charts and we did a Top of the Pops, Elton sent us a crate of pink champagne along with a letter.

In 1980, communication was very different to now! There were no mobile phones and no instant messages. The quickest

Love,
Elton

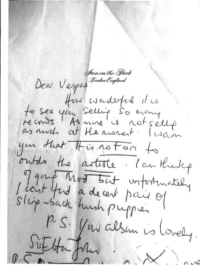

Elton's letter and card that went with the champagne

22

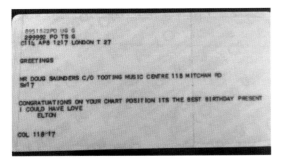
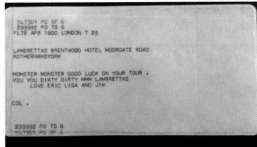

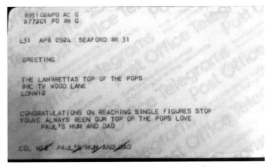

Telegrams

way of getting a message to someone was by telegram, and they were used quite a bit for congratulations

Their third single 'D-a-a-ance' was released on 15th May. This was a picture disc with the Union Flag on the A-side, and on the B-side; 'Can't You Feel the Beat' was a picture of Brighton Palace Pier.

'D-a-a-ance' got to number 12 in the UK singles charts. It was so much more popular than the distributor envisaged that they temporarily ran out of stocks.

Dance Picture Disc

They were on Top Of The Pops playing 'D-a-a-ance' on 22 May 1980.

Fiona: Jez and I met when I was 17. We shared the same home town. He was prolific with his song writing at that time and most of his songs were composed on his Levin acoustic guitar. He would then come visit and play them to me over a cup of tea and cake!

To quote Jez: "*Lots of the songs are love songs and some have very serious lyrics which I try to deliver as clearly as possible. I think it's important to feel like you're saying it to somebody.*"

Doug: I'm often being asked why and how our songs came about. Jez and I wrote together and separately. The lyrical and musical content of some of the songs was what we thought to be relevant to the times. However, one song that comes to mind is 'Listen Listen Listen', which Jez and I wrote early on.

See the men of reason, Smiling on the box
Rebounding from their critics, See them take the knocks
Smooth in smug assurance they talk in quiet tones
The skin in which they're packaged conceals their jagged bones

Confront them with the truth, And they recoil in mock surprise
Don't be taken in, they only tell us lies

Listen, Listen, Listen, but don't believe them

Cool behind the cameras, Their well-fed faces gleam
You never see the other side, That remains unseen
Pressure from the outside, Is all that we can do
Reveal them in their true light, It's up to me and you

It's obviously about politicians, and we thought at the time it was current and relevant to the times it was written. Mrs Thatcher's Conservative party had just won the general election on 3rd May 1979, and Britain was certainly changing. Being a fairly ardent follower of political articles and programmes, both then and now, especially the likes of Question Time, one can't help noticing in 2020 the same old questions, evasive answers, and various agendas, that nothing has changed. At that time, we naively thought it might. Maybe one day!

By contrast, the song 'Ambience', an instrumental, was a nod to Lowell George, an artist with a really soulful voice, a great slide guitar player, and someone who I still listen to now, despite being gone for so long.

A company I once worked for had an account slip to be delivered if there was no-one at home. It said "*I called on you today to settle your account*". Jez and I thought it was a good idea as an opening line, so we changed 'your' to 'my', and the lyrics to Runaround were born.

'Living for Today' wasn't a mind bogglingly deep song lyric, just a simple observation on young people that I noticed at on my travels, and what was important to them. Much the same as young folk anywhere, anytime I imagine. Another later song, 'Decent Town' was more or less the same, but based more specifically on a couple of local lovable rogues I knew.

A lot of Lambrettas songs I think, had quite good lyrics, not necessarily the standard throw-away pop song. One of my favourites is Jez's words to 'Page 3'. Very cynical, very funny and even today I'm not quite sure everyone gets it.

Jez and I wrote various songs together, all with the band in mind, but after a time we decided to create some words by cutting up adverts and articles from newspapers and magazines and putting them all into a hat to create a story. One of us had read that David Bowie used this method once or twice, (whether it is true or not I don't know but it worked for us). The song was called 'I Wish I Lived in Paris', and was recorded as a single by a girl called Diane Mulvey. Not much of a pop star name, and I think the label had a small budget, so it got lost in the torrent of singles being released in the early eighties. We reunited again with Peter Haines to work on this single. I've often wondered about resurrecting it. The chorus was

Take me back to the desert where the pyramids end
I wanna capture Egyptians in my Japanese lens
Maybe a night at the Opera and a metro home
A view of the Seine from a room of my own
.... I wish I lived in Paris

I mentioned Beat Boys earlier, so enough of songwriting for now!

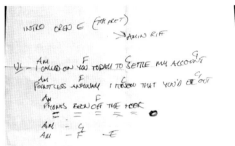

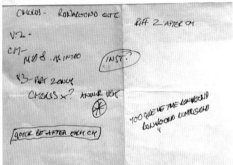

Doug's songwriting notes 1979

Diane Mulvey

25

Radio airplay in the 70's and 80's was everything for a band. The Lambrettas remember that the Radio 1 DJ, Mike Read was the first radio DJ to champion them. He played Go Steady on his Saturday evening show on Radio 1. They were also on his play list both for 'Poison Ivy' and 'D-a-a-ance', and their paths crossed quite frequently in the early 1980's.

They were back at The Marquee on 24th June 1980, and at the end of their set, Mike came on stage and presented them with silver discs for 'Poison Ivy'! Afterwards they all went out to dinner with Mike, Pete Waterman, Peter Collins and John Reid who at the time was Elton's business partner and joint-owner of Rocket Records.

BACK *L-R: Peter Collins, John Hall, Sally Atkins, John Reid, Paul* FRONT *L-R: Doug, Mark, Jez*

BACK *L-R: Peter Collins, Mike Read, Pete Waterman* FRONT *L-R: Paul, Doug, Mark, Jez*

BACK *L-R: John Reid, Peter Haines, Mike Read* FRONT *L-R: Paul, Doug, Mark, Jez*

L-R: Lyn, Amanda, Doug, Mark, John Reid, Shelley, Jez, Paul

AT THE BACK STANDING *L-R: Mike Read, John Reid* SITTING *L-R: Paul, Peter Haines, Doug, Mark, Jez*

Pete Waterman: The night of the silver disc presentations was another time when me and Peter smoked big fat cigars. These were our first silver discs. **There we were in an Italian restaurant with The Lambrettas and Rocket Records smoking cigars.**

It was a turning point for mine and Peter's careers. It was fate really and it started to take off for us after that. We worked together for a few more years, and then Peter went to live and work in America, and I carried on here.

Peter Haines: 'Poison Ivy' was a great cover. I loved receiving the silver disc. Rocket organised the presentation, and we went out to celebrate after with the band, crew and people from Rocket.

Willie Bourne (Friend of Jez): I went to see the Lambrettas at the Marquee Club with Pete Westbrook in 1980. Mike Read came along to present a silver disc for 'Poison Ivy'. Pete and I were roped in to help with keeping people off the stage as semi-skilled boozed up bouncers (we had had a few during sound checks). After the presentation the band launched into playing the song and mods leapt onto the stage. I took my assigned role quite seriously and started to get people off the stage. In doing so I tried to push Mike Read off the stage, "Not me you fool – I'm Mike Read" Oops!! Next night I listened to his show where he said he had a great night at the Marquee Lambrettas gig but a bit manic as "*some bouncer tried to throw me offstage!*"

Just a week later, on 1st July, they were at The Marquee again. This time they filmed a promo video for their next single 'Page 3'. They also did some photo shoots for magazines that afternoon as well.

Magazine pics

Another person who really looked out for The Lambrettas was their music publisher at Rocket Music, Eric Hall. They all have fond memories of Eric.

Paul: He used to take us out to places on Rocket's expense account. One of our favourite places was a club called 'Legends Nightclub and Restaurant' in Mayfair.

Awards ceremonies didn't really happen much in 1980! For example, 'The Brits' didn't originate as an annual event until 1982. On 30th September Eric took Doug, Jez, Amanda and Fiona to the Tin Pan Alley Ball at the London Hilton in Park Lane.

AT THE BACK STANDING: *Eric Hall*
IN FRONT OF ERIC L-R: *Wayne Sleep, Doug, Jez, ?, Chris Quentin*

Legends matchboxes

Tin Pan Alley Ball programme, table seating card & matchbook

Fiona: This was an event for music publishers and was a very corporate thing at that time, but we still had a laugh. While there we shared a table with quite a few publishers and also the dancer Wayne Sleep, and a guy called Chris Quentin (Brian in Coronation Street). One of the waiters asked Jez for his autograph, and Amanda asked him who he thought Jez was…the answer? – Sandy from Crossroads! Jez never lived it down! After the ball we went to Legends with Eric and Chris, then on to the Cavendish Hotel for an early breakfast, and then back to Eric's house in Star Street to get a bit of sleep.

Amanda: Eric championed The Lambrettas from the start. I remember being in his office one day when Poison Ivy was just starting to go up the charts. Jez said it would be nice to get on Top of The Pops, Eric made a phone call, and then rang off and said you're on next Thursday, get to studios on the Wednesday to record it. He just always used to make stuff happen! I used to love going out with him, he proper looked after us and he always made me laugh! Another memorable night was in Nottingham. The Lambrettas were in the middle of a British tour, and were playing at The Theatre Royal on Wednesday 23 July 1980. ATV televised the gig and it was shown later on TV as part of a series called Rockstage, with a different band on each week. Me and Fiona drove up to meet up with them and stay overnight. It was a great gig, but I think all the mods got over excited on the way home, as the next day it was in the local paper with the heading 'Mobs clash after city pop concert'. I remember Eric came up and we all sat in a box at the theatre, something I'd never done before, and then he took us out to dinner after.

MOBS CLASH AFTER CITY POP CONCERT

RIGHT: *Nottingham newspaper*

By Colin Meakin

NOTTINGHAM was cleaning up today after rival gangs of Punks, Mods and Rockers clashed in the city centre. Windows were smashed, cars damaged, and motorcycles kicked over — bringing seven arrests by police.

Trouble began at about 10pm as hundreds of Mods filed out of the Theatre Royal after what had been a peaceful concert by the The Lambrettas pop group.

Out of control

Fights among small groups broke out and as police swooped huge bands of Mods ran away from the scene towards Market Square.

As the youths ran out of control, windows were smashed, seats upturned and scuffles broke out between the Mods and their rivals, the Punks and Rockers.

An eyewitness said today: "As the Mods were leaving the Theatre Royal hundreds of them began stampeding towards Market Square.

"I heard one of them shout about The Imperial pub in St. James Street and many of them ran in that direction."

Mr. Terry Rayns, manager of The Imperial, was outside his pub as a gang of 40 Mods appeared. "They came from nowhere chasing two youths up St. James Street. They were shouting 'We Are The Mods'. They tried to get into my pub, but I told them to clear off.

"They began fighting and throwing glasses and bottles about.

"A group of them forced me in ....

ABOVE: *L-R: Jez, Eric Hall, Doug, Paul, Mark*

RIGHT: *Nottingham Flyer*

LAMBRETAS

Supported by BILLY KARLOFF AND THE EXTREMES

JULY 23rd – 7.30
Seat Prices – £2, £1.50, £1

THEATRE ROYAL Theatre Square Nottingham Telephone 0602 42328 9

Doug: I still speak to him from time to time. He went on to become a football agent after the music business, and now presents a Radio show in Essex on Sunday afternoons. Some of his sayings are legendary: "*Never change a winning act*", "*A friend in need is a pest*", "*Many a true word spoke in court*", and obviously the one he is most famous for is "*Monster, Monster*". He left Rocket Records around end 1980, beginning 1981, I think.

The album 'Beat Boys in the Jet Age' was recorded at TMC Studios in Tooting, and was produced by Peter Collins, with Pete Waterman coming in most days as well. Their engineer was Pete Hammond, and they spent the spring of 1980 travelling up to Tooting whenever they were free from gigs to get all the songs recorded and mixed.

29

ABOVE: *Inside TMC*

the Chart

This week's musician's choice by:

Peter Collins

— musician (guitar & keyboards), writer and now leading independent producer. Former Decca recording artist. Key figure in current rockabilly boom — produced Matchbox hits 'Rockabilly Rebel' and new chart success 'Buzz Buss A Diddle It'.

SINGLES
1 You've Been Talking In Your Sleep — Crystal Gale — UA
2 Pop Musik — M — MCA
3 Living By Numbers — New Musik — GTO
4 Oliver's Army — Elvis Costello — Radar
5 Go Steady — Lambrettas — Rocket
6 Girls Talk — Dave Edmunds — Swan Song
7 Lucky Number — Lene Lovich — Stiff
8 A Walk In The Park — Nick Straker Band — Pinnacle
9 She's In Love With You — Suzi Quatro — Rak
10 Heart of Glass — Blondie — Chrysalis

ALBUMS
1 Repeat When Necessary — Dave Edmunds — Swan Song
2 The Fine Art Of Surfacing — Boomtown Rats — Ensign
3 Labour Of Lust — Nick Lowe — Radar
4 Dire Straits — Dire Straits — Mercury
5 New Boots & Panties — Ian Drury — Stiff
6 Regatta De Blanc — Police — A&M
7 Parallel Lines — Blondie — Chrysalis
8 Voulez-Vous — Abba — CBS
9 Breakfast In America — Supertramp — A&M
10 Look Sharp — Joe Jackson — A&M

So, there were 3 Peter's involved in the making of Beat Boys. Luckily engineer Pete and producer Peter liked each other and got on very well, which is always a bonus when working so closely for a few months at a time. Pete Waterman was there as well, but not as much as the other two were.

Amanda: I was lucky enough to catch up with Peter Collins on the phone in July 2020 and he said the following.

Peter Collins: 'Poison Ivy' was my second ever hit, the first being 'Rockabilly Rebel' by Matchbox. When I went to work with Matchbox, I used to wear a 10-gallon hat and cowboy boots, etc. Then when I went to work with the Lambrettas I had to tone down all the rockabilly stuff. It was a bit like Superman — doing a quick change in a phone booth, and on to the next band!

However, it established a pattern for me that stood me in good stead for the future. I could produce bands of lots of different genres, rather than being tied down to working with one type of band. It was a pivotal grounding, and made it much less limiting for me as a producer.

About the band; I remember all the characters pretty well. Jez being full of beans; he was a really good writer. Doug; great guitar and was always a cool cat. (I've looked at a couple of vids online from the last 10 years, and as a lead singer he has a bit of attitude). Paul; good drummer, tight, solid and very effective. Mark; solid bass player and questioned everything.

I regularly go Tango dancing. We do 3 dances, then there is a short gap between, to give time to go back to the table and choose a new dance partner before starting the next 3 dances, this gap is called a Cortina. So, every week when I go dancing, I think of The Lambrettas; "*She gives him love on the leatherette…but she only loves him because he's got a Cortina!*"

My first silver disc was 'Poison Ivy', and it was my first hit with Pete Waterman. Pete had a lot of concepts and picked the artists and I produced them. It was a good partnership and I enjoyed working with him, as I did with The Lambrettas. When you hear the music today, I think it stands the test of time, and I'm very proud of it. Thank you for the memories. **You don't stop dancing because you get old, you get old because you stop dancing.**

Peter Collins went on to produce Nik Kershaw, Musical Youth, Tracey Ullman, Alvin Stardust, and others with Pete Waterman. Then he moved to the States in 1985 where he stayed, working with Gary Moore, Bon Jovi, Rush and Alice Cooper among others.

This is an extract on The Lambrettas taken from Pete Hammond's book:

As we were leaving the studio after the session Peter Collins took me to one side and said,

"Pete, we need to book some more time with you…Heir Wasserman (as he always referred to Waterman) wants me to record another band from Brighton. You're going to have to help me out on this one, Pete; apparently they are a new 'Mod' band, and I'm a Rockabilly producer; I haven't got a clue what to do…"

"No problem, don't worry," I said confidently, "we'll cope alright." Although the truth was, I had no idea what to do either!

The Mod band was called The Lambrettas…and they were mad! Every so often during recording sessions the lead guitarist would take great delight in dropping to the floor, lying on his back with his legs over his head, whilst striking a match. He would then put the lighted match near his bum – and fart! His jeans would then take on an appearance similar to that of a lighted Christmas pudding, with blue gaseous flames flickering around his buttocks.

The picture of The Lambrettas was taken on the rear fire escape at TMC Studios. You can just see the door on the right at the top of the stairs that led to the drum booth. (*See prelims page VIII for picture.*)

Doug: In my defence it sounds like I've dedicated my life to lighting farts, whereas I think it was more likely an isolated session. However, any young bands reading this, it is an integral part of the recording process.

The band also had to do some photo sessions for the artwork and covers of Beat Boys.

Laura Croker: The idea evolved for the cover of what was to be 'Beat Boys in the Jet Age'. We ended up on Camber Sands with a load of small TV monitors which we had hired from a facilities house. We set them up in racks on the beach, and then dug a big hole nearby and sunk a galvanised dustbin into the sand. Mark climbed out of the dustbin as if he were escaping into this new world of television screens – at least, I think that was the concept. I remember being rather nervous about returning the screens to the facilities house in case they were impaired by all the sand, but we got away with it.

Doug: One of the sessions we had to do for Beat Boys was at Camber Sands. We all travelled there together in one car with Derek driving us as usual, and Rocket and the company who were doing the photos all arrived in separate transport. They brought props with them, some of which were the mirror sunglasses that we are wearing on the front cover photos. They handed out the sunglasses and told us to be careful with them as they were expensive, and they said *"Make sure you give them back to us as soon as you've finished."* Anyway, we all rather liked them, so when the session finished, we got back into the car, locked all the doors, put on the sunglasses, Derek tooted the horn, we all put up two fingers and waved goodbye, with them chasing us and shaking their fists. We thought it was hilarious, but probably the bill just went to Rocket anyway!

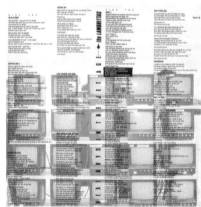

'Beat Boys in the Jet Age' was released in June 1980, and was in the album charts for quite some time, peaking at number 28. It has always had pretty rave reviews, although probably more so in retrospect than at the time in 1980.

The following review about Beat Boys in the Jet Age, was taken from Amazon:

5.0 out of 5 stars Cracking Tunes From Pop Geniuses, 18 Jan 2002. By A Customer.
"When the NME writers got together in 1989 to list their top 100 of the albums of the 1980's – Who would have thought a 79 Mod band would be in there alongside U2 and Bruce Springsteen? Beat Boys In The Jet Age is one of the best pop albums ever made, with one of the most imaginative sleeves. The Lambrettas would have worked on any audience, they didn't need the mod credentials as a crutch. What a bonus we mods got them as our band."

Music papers didn't often give very good reviews around 1980. The Lambrettas suffered from their bad reviews quite regularly, although it didn't stop their fans from buying their records or going to their gigs.

Letter from A Fan

Paris

Paul: A journalist from Sounds was sent to Paris to spend the day with us and was told to come and spend as much of our money as he could, and then do a hatchet job on us! After spending time with us, he decided that we were actually ok, so he toned down the review he was going to publish.

Paul, Jez & Doug
up the Eiffel Tower

Derek in Paris

Doug in Paris

Mark: Most people I knew were happy for our success. But I remember every now and then I'd be in a pub, at a party, and someone would launch into an attack on me for the band 'selling out'. Apparently to some people the one thing a band must not do is be successful.

Andrew Gilbert: I must have seen The Lambrettas around 20 times in London between '79 – '82. There are three shows that stand out, all from 1980 and within a few weeks of each other.

Friday 28th March 1980, I rush home from school, I was only 15, run to Upton Park tube, change at Mile End and meet up with Martin Smith, Ed Piller and Tris Pitt on the platform before getting the Central line to Tottenham Court Road. The YMCA was a tower block in the back streets and we weren't expecting to have to go up in a lift to the venue, it was like 'Room at The Top' in Ilford. Arriving early to make sure we got all the bands in; The Agents, The Small Hours and of course The Lambrettas. It was always a gamble whether we would make the last tube back towards home so we hoped it didn't finish later than 11.

I remember it being extremely hot in the venue, the stage being in the corner, a low ceiling and the bar in another room. Can't remember much about The Agents, I was probably in the bar but The Small Hours were great….'soul shoes on my feet, I've got soul shoes on my feet'.

The heat was certainly turned up when The Lambrettas came on, the place was heaving! Six days earlier they had been on TISWAS, essential Saturday morning viewing back then, and it had put numbers on the door.

Everyone sang along as if their lives depended on it. When 'Poison Ivy' started, stage invasion and the next thing I know I was jumping about by the floor tom and just couldn't resist picking up a drum stick whilst Paul wasn't looking. I waited for my chance to hit the cowbell. Mission accomplished.

Tuesday 24th June 1980, school night, but that didn't stop us, ever! The Marquee was a very special place. We missed the support I think, Vogue, as the queue outside was silly. Keeping an eye out for skinheads and others looking to ruin our night, but with it being a Tuesday they had stayed away. The Lambrettas didn't disappoint, Jez Bird was a great front man, energetic, engaging and eyeliner. Towards the end of the set Mike Read, (no not that one from Runaround) appears from the dressing room door. Cue another stage invasion and, as if by magic, I am standing outside the DJ booth while the band get presented with a silver disc for 'Poison Ivy'. There was the opportunity, I had the drum stick, now there was a guitar on a stand right next to me. I acquired Doug's nice white guitar strap, and still have it.

Saturday 9th August 1980, Martin, Ed and myself had spent the afternoon at Wembley watching an awful Charity Shield; Liverpool v West Ham. The most memorable part was bumping into Derwent Jaconelli, he was handing out flyers for the upcoming England v Scotland match and were we interested in being part of the 'firm'. We get the tube back towards Camden to meet up with James van Lint and Tris amongst others, if I remember. The wonderful Music Machine, now a burnt-out shell, was tonight's venue for The Lambrettas and Daddy Yum Yum. Just two months earlier The Lambrettas had played just down the road at The Electric Ballroom supported by The VIPs, the wonderful Dolly Mixture and Godz Toys, who seemed to support almost everyone. An afternoon of football, an evening of cheap lager and a sweaty venue meant we were looking forward to getting home. However, some of the locals had a different idea. As we left the show by the front door, turned right towards Camden Town tube, we were met by a group of skinheads who chased us towards the station. More appeared in from behind a newspaper stand, Ed got kicked in the stomach as we ran past for our lives. There were more waiting at the tube station so we headed off towards Holloway Road. Those heavy Doc Martens and days of sniffing glue slowed them down and we

LEFT AND ABOVE: *Tickets*

RIGHT: *Andrew Gilbert 1980*

were soon wandering the back streets towards Finsbury Park station, too late – it was closed! So, more walking down the Seven Sisters Road, prompting choruses of 'Saturday Night Beneath the Plastic Palm Trees'. We decided to head towards Hackney and hopefully we could get a train or bus from there. Through Stamford Hill, Stoke Newington and on towards Clapton, where we followed a trail of blood on the pavement before deciding it might not be good idea. Our parents had no idea where we were and neither did we. We carried on walking through the night and ended up at The Blind Beggar as the sun came up, knackered. Another memorable night with The Lambrettas.

Andrew Gilbert, aged 54 and 3/4.

Laura Croker: Before we had decided on the name and cover for 'Beat Boys', we did a photo session with the band on Brighton beach in front of the merchant ship Athina B, which had beached near the Palace Pier due to engine failure and was causing quite a stir. At the time we were thinking of images for the first album cover and I suggested using these photos and calling the album 'Attention All Shipping', but nobody liked the idea. I think the band were too cool to be associated with anything that had a Radio 4 connection!

After Beat Boys was released, they carried on gigging over the summer, along with radio interviews and some TV appearances. Here are some of their publicity photos

Around this time Peter Haines decided to move on from The Lambrettas. He was replaced by Ike Nossel, who had known The Lambrettas for a few years. Ike, as well as owning and running a recording studio, was a musician and a songwriter, and one of his songs had previously been recorded by Shakedown.

Ike: I had originally trained as a tape op and engineer at Abbey Road in the mid-seventies. I then freelanced, mainly in Germany. A few lucky breaks meant I had the luxury of being able to build my own studio. In mid-1978 I found a set of buildings in Catsfield village, a mile south of Battle, where King Harold met his fate in 1066. The main studio building was a 3,400 sq. ft high roofed Sussex Barn, which had been built as stables. It still had the horse stalls in it. Just over nine months later it was open for business. Our first client was Wreckless Eric for Stiff Records. The client however who put us on the map to lead the studio to become one of the premier residential studios in Europe, was Paul McCartney, who was in the studio for almost two years, with a few breaks in between.

Inside Parkgate Studio

Doug: When in Shakedown we recorded a song that Ike wrote called 'FBI'. It was released as a single. We were young and inexperienced, and it ended up sounding some-what bland, which was a shame as it could have been so much more if we had known

a bit about production at that time. It was released on a label called Kricon by a company owned by James Chrimes, a lovely soul and friend of our Roadie Derek Haggar. Sadly, James passed away very recently in 2020, but we had fun and he will always be in our memories.

Ike took over from Peter Haines around July 1980.

Ike: I had known Doug and Amanda since the late seventies. I grew up in Brighton and they lived in nearby Lewes. The music scene was still small back then, so it was inevitable almost everyone involved knew each other. The Lambrettas had signed to Elton John and John Reid's Rocket Records Label. A while after they got to no 7 in the charts with 'Poison Ivy', Doug approached me and asked me if I was interested in managing them. Management until that point, wasn't really my "thing" but I "gave it a go".

Amanda: Ike helped us to co-ordinate all the Fan Club paraphernalia into one place. I had been running the fan club from home, but Rocket Records had been receiving fan letters at their offices as well, and press agents had been replying but we weren't tying things together. We organised a trip to Rocket to collect all their stuff and joined it together with ours. We have some friends now who were members of the fan club then, and they asked me why I chose to call myself Jo. I don't really know except times were different then, and the record company didn't really want fans to know I was Doug's wife. Jez did the artwork on the back of my hand written letter, and we got them printed

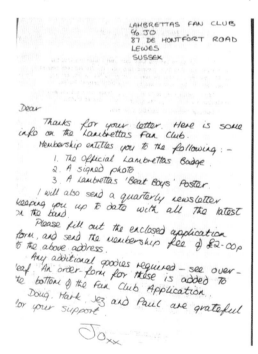

Fan Club letter

Fan club merch

Badges   *Birthday card that Jez made for Doug*

up. Jez was actually a really good artist, and he would sometimes escape by himself and sit and draw. I think he found it relaxing. We were always given his drawings on birthday cards. We didn't sell merchandise at gigs then, just through the Fan Club.

Around this time, they went to Manchester to visit Holcombe Manor and take part in the Krypton Factor assault course. There was an idea to put some bands through the course and then show it on a clips programme, or to advertise the show. In the end this never happened, but The Lambrettas did complete the course.

Doug: When we were at the Krypton Factor there were about 10 obstacles. The final one was a very high and long zip wire. There were soldiers around the course just for safety. I was the last person on the zip wire. Once I had put my hands in the straps the soldiers went to push me off and pulled my track suit trousers down to my ankles.

At the Krypton Factor

Everyone thought it was hilarious! Embarrassment and being really annoyed didn't even cover it, although had it been anyone else, I'm sure I would have joined in the laughter. No doubt at the time I'm sure I thought I was the coolest band member and no-one would pull a stunt like that on me. Looking back, hindsight being the wonderful thing it is, it was excellent, at my expense, but excellent nevertheless.

A few of the more light hearted articles and pictures of The Lambrettas…

Fans meeting The Lambrettas and Elton John

Magazine pics

Mark: Not sure where, but we were staying at a country hotel. Doug and I were both up early, and going outside for a smoke spotted a tethered goat on the lawn. I don't know how it came about, but we wanted to test the goat's reputation for being able to consume almost anything. So, of course we fed it a cigarette or two, then the whole lot, including the pack. I wonder now, could that amount of nicotine kill a beast that size? I guess I'll never know!

They did a couple more TV shows to promote their new single 'Page 3' which was released on 1st August 1980. A few things happened at this stage that were beyond their control, which possibly contributed to them not going further in their career at that stage!

Sally Atkins: We were up against a powerful antagonist when The Sun decided that the band was 'passing off' I believe was the term, with their 'Page 3' single. I thought it was one of Jez's more inspired titles and lyrics, but the record had to be withdrawn and re-issued as 'Another Day, Another Girl'.

The Sun newspaper took them to court and a High Court judge granted an injunction to ban the release of the single under the name 'Page 3'. He wouldn't ban the Beat Boys album though, so this was why the song was called 'Page 3' on the album. This meant they had to quickly re-name and re-package the single and call it 'Another Day, Another Girl'.

Original Page 3 cover   *Another Day cover*

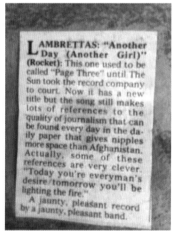

Newspapers

As well as the problems with the injunction holding up the release of their 4th single, the Musicians Union (MU) went on strike which meant that although they went and recorded a video for TOTPs on 27th August 1980, this never aired.

Mark: For TV programs, bands were supposed to re-record their songs for the show, because in earlier years acts/singers would usually have session players who wanted to get paid for TV appearances; in other words, if you weren't going to play live, but mime, then a re-recording guaranteed work for session musicians. In practice, all that happened by the period we were doing shows, is that recording studio time was booked a couple of nights before, we all sat around doing nothing, and a tape of the original song was presented to the BBC for us to mime to, but the session players technically still had work. At the time 'Page 3' was out, the MU were on strike. Because of those arrangements, it meant that as far as they were concerned, if a band recorded songs for a show, the session players were unavailable as they were striking. So, the farce of pretending to use them couldn't go on. The Beeb had that week's TOTP recorded in the hope that the strike would be resolved. It wasn't, and so the entire show was shelved. That really was what ended our momentum; I feel if that TOTP had aired, I think we would have had another hit.

'Another Day, Another Girl' only got to number 49 in the UK charts. This was on 2nd September, and it was believed that had the TOTPs aired it would have gone higher, and perhaps things might have been different for The Lambrettas.

They did however go to ITV/Granada studios in Manchester and filmed a Live performance of 'Page 3', which aired on the ITV pop programme called Fun Factory on 23rd August.

Fun Factory

Doug: We also did some other TV shows in Europe, but I can't remember what they were, Mark might remember?

Mark: The only European TV I recall was Stockholm, Sweden, November 3, 1980, on the tour with Madness. Also appearing: Pat Benatar, Lynton Quasi Johnson, Julie Felix. We played live for real. We did 'D-a-a-ance', and 'London Calling'. The tape is available at an institution in Sweden. Would be great to see! I have the running script from the show.

Doug: On one of our tours around the UK in 1980, we were approached by two skinheads asking if they could have a job. They were from East Grinstead and were called Chris and Ive. They wore bleached levis, DMs, the whole kit. We said they could come with us for a few days and help Derek roadie and do a bit of stage security. They were in fact really gentle souls with no malice whatsoever and we had some real laughs with them. One gig in Bath had an audience of mostly teenage mods, but stood at the back were about 50 skinheads with a very different agenda to Chris and Ive. We asked them to keep an eye on the situation while we played, but they said *"We're not going out there, there's loads of skinheads!"* Jez told me in the early noughties he ran into Chris in East Grinstead, they recognised each other and he told Jez that those days were among the best he'd ever had. It made me quite nostalgic I have to say. I really hope wherever they are they're doing good.

Derek: At the beginning of August 1980, I got told we're doing a gig in Douglas, Isle of Man. Oh and you need to take the guitars because the guys are flying. Ok I said but I'm gonna need a hand. That's ok they said, do you know anyone? Not offhand I said but I'll try to find someone. When are we going? You're booked on the I O M ferry from Heysham tonight they said. Right-ho says I, and went and borrowed my Mum's car. Having collected the gear, I went in search of an assistant. Where to look? The Lamb pub in Lewes of course! There are always people in there of a lunchtime, and sure enough in walks recently married Tim Bradfield. Want to come to the IOM I ask. When says he, now says I; free beer and grub. Ok he says! Bear in mind this is before mobile phones and he's told his new Missus he's popping out for a paper. So off we go to get a ferry north of Liverpool! We get there eventually, park the car and lug the gear on the ferry, and despite the rough crossing we get to Douglas. I had to share my room with Tim and his snoring! Next day we did the gig, and afterwards went back to the hotel bar and drank far too much. Next morning, I woke to Tim's snoring again, saw the time and realised we had five minutes to get the ferry. We sat on the dock watching the ferry disappear over the horizon. Having made enquires we found out there were no more ferries to Heysham for a few days, but we could get on the one to Liverpool in an hour. Once on board, I noticed an unearthly smell coming from my case. Turns out Tim had taken his socks off (that he'd had on for three days), and put them in my bag for safe keeping. After a few expletives I got them out and threw them overboard. They're probably still swimming round the Irish Sea. Eventually we got to Liverpool only to find we had to get a taxi north for 50 miles to get back to the car. I'm not sure what Cass, Tim's missus said when he arrived home 3 days after going out to get a paper!

All the Tours that the Lambrettas went on, both in the UK and Europe were organised for them by The Bron Agency. Everyone was given a personal itinerary with all necessary travel, hotel, venue, interviews, etc. info. The bands very rarely referred to them, they just waited for the Tour Manager to tell them what to do.

In October 1980 they went on tour in Europe with Madness. Derek drove them and dealt with all their equipment as usual, and another guy travelled with them as their Tour Manager. He was called Gem, and had previously worked for and dated Toyah.

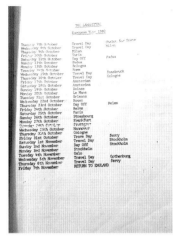

Derek and No.1 helper Matty

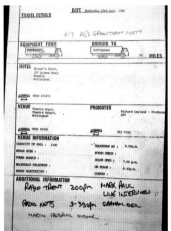

Paul: So, we pulled into our hotel someplace in Germany. I don't remember exactly where, and next to the hotel there was a drive-in movie in full flow. Excited by this I got straight to my room and went to fling the window open for a better view. Unbeknown to me, it was one of those windows that only opened a few inches, and because I'd used a fair bit of force, the glass cracked from corner to corner! I was sharing with Mark Ellis in the same room. He flipped out and jumped up and down on the waste bin and also stole the pillow. We were now officially 'The Who' in my mind!

Derek: So many memories from that Madness tour. We were sat in the bar of the American hotel in Amsterdam on a night off having driven from Rome in 2 days, when Suggs and the other one came in looking pissed off. On enquiring, we discovered they wanted to spend their evening off having a few beers with the "Rockin Lambos", as they called us. But were being dragged out on a press meet and greet on an Amsterdam canal boat. Off they duly went with much umbrage, only to return about half an hour later in a much better mood. Apparently, they had snuck out of the press room and

Somewhere in Europe

L-R: Derek, Jez, Doug, Paul   *Doug, Derek, Gem, Jez*

Somewhere in Europe

onto the roof of the canal boat. As it passed under one of the bridges they managed to get up onto the bridge and then legged it back to the hotel. Of course, their management thought they had gone overboard into the canal. They called out the emergency services who spent ages trying to find them. When they were discovered in the bar, the proverbial hit the fan. I gather their Tour Manager Kellogs was not amused.

Paul: So, we somehow got roped into playing live on Swedish tv on their big Saturday night show, whatever that may have been. We had already played a pretty exhausting set opening for Madness at the local super mega Hyperdome type thing, and then got whisked away to this TV studio. So, there I was sat behind this rickety old drum kit that belonged to the house band thinking; "this'll be interesting then". So, what happened was that the Compere was telling Swedish jokes etc and we were told that when there's a huge round of applause you guys start. Big applause happens, I count us in and we're off. We all had rubbish gear to use and it was all a bit messy and we were all still pumped up after the gig. As the song progressed, I was hitting harder and harder on this poor old kit and all of sudden a cymbal fell with the stand still attached. Well for me this was a cue to be Keith Moon! More cymbals went, as I pushed the buggers over, and what was left of the kit was a bit of a mess. To top it off, apparently, we had started half way though the Compere's best joke!

Mark: The tour with Madness was an incredible experience. I had a lot of fun, the gigs were great, Madness were brilliant to watch, and they were decent guys. In Oslo on the last night of the tour, Suggs came on stage with us and sang along with 'Poison Ivy'. When Madness were doing their encore later, we invaded the stage, wearing silly masks, and shooting at them with water pistols. It was a lot of fun. Looking back, probably not the best idea to be spraying water around all those microphones, amplifiers, etc. But we survived!

The last gig in the European tour with Madness was in Norway on 4th November. They

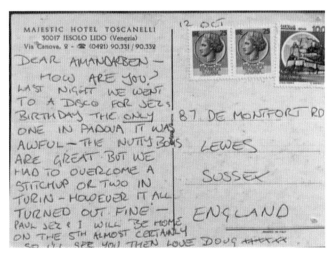

LEFT: *Postcard from Doug*

ABOVE: *Lewes Bonfire Celebrations*

47

had all been travelling in the van together, but Doug, Jez and Paul got a plane back first thing on Wednesday 5th as it was bonfire night, and Lewes people don't like to miss the bonfire celebrations!

Derek: I travelled back from Europe on the ferry with Mark, Gem, the van and some of the Madness crew. Mark hated flying, and so avoided it whenever possible, but the other three wanted to get back for Bonfire Night.

Ferry back from Europe

There were only a couple more gigs in 1980 after the Madness tour, and a bit of time off over Christmas.

Amanda: I remember going to the Rocket Christmas party on 23rd December! In 1980 the variety of foods weren't available like they are now! I remember being very impressed with the big prawns! There were a lot of old school cigar smoking music business people there. In retrospect, although we thought they were old fashioned and not in the know, they all knew exactly what they were doing, and the music business was a better place then! I also remember there was a guy there called Paul, who we

Rocket Records Christmas Present

were friends with. He was John Reid's boyfriend, and he said "*Have a look out of the window at my Christmas present!*" It was a red soft top Mercedes sports car. We got a Christmas present of a pink Rocket Records sports car, but it was a china ashtray! Not quite the same as Paul's present, but I love it and we still have it today!

The plan had then been to go to America at the beginning of 1981 as support to Ultravox, but Rocket decided they wanted another album to be recorded first. So as soon as Christmas was over, they were back in the studio recording their second album, which would be called 'Ambience'. This time it was at Parkgate Studios in Catsfield, near Hastings, and it was owned by Ike. They all went to a Parkgate New Years' Eve party, and then on 1st January they got down to recording. This time their producer was Steve James, Sid James (the actor's) son. Steve had been suggested by Ike as he had been working at Parkgate previously producing Toyah.

Steve James at Parkgate

Peter Haines: When I was in California some years later, I was amazed to find the mod revival was bigger and more developed almost than here. So, I think The Lambrettas should have gone there and to Canada without a doubt!

For a little while they had been having a few musical differences, and Paul was particularly struggling, and so, sadly on Saturday 10th January 1981, after only recording just one track ('Good Times'), Paul decided to split from them to go and do his own thing. The last gig he played in that era was Margate on 17th January 1981. For a very short time the replacement drummer was Steve Bray, who had been Toyah's drummer up until 1980.

Eddie Piller: I'd been a fan of the Lambrettas since the very earliest days – we'd caught them live at one of their first London pub gigs with The Scooters at The Wellington, a mod stronghold in Waterloo and from then on made it a priority to follow the band from gig to gig. They were friendly and generous with their time and we would make a point of getting to venues early to take in the soundcheck.

I'd featured them in my fanzine Extraordinary Sensations on a number of occasions and am one of the young mods pictured during the stage invasion at the Marquee Club in Wardour Street that's featured on the front cover of their debut single, Go Steady.

Jez Bird and Doug Sanders had given me their numbers so I could phone up if I ever wanted to make a sound check or have a guest list – I was chuffed.

Consequently on a blustery mid-January morning in 1981 I met up with fellow fanzine editor Steve Road-runner and a group of four other mates from South London – Rick The Kip, so named because he was always falling asleep on our away-day journeys, Irish

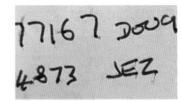

Doug and Jez's numbers given to Ed Piller

Gerry (who wasn't actually Irish), Nick The Comb from Eltham and my beautiful girl-friend Sandra O'Shea from Stockwell. I specifically remember that three of us were wearing trench coats, mine was brown leather, Sandra's was a short beige three-quarter length and Gerry's was just like the one pioneered by Gary Shail's character Spider in

49

Quadrophenia!

Margate was in (what we thought at the time) terminal decline. This was long before the re-gentrification of British seaside towns that began with Brighton's make-over in the early 2000's. Back in '81 it was a semi derelict, depressing place with grey, dirty streets, shuttered amusement arcades and…er…skinheads.

We'd all met up at King's Cross at midday with half a dozen cans of Skol and some Cider, enthusing about our trip and although the rain lashing against the carriage window should have blunted our enthusiasm, it didn't. An hour and a half later we disembarked from the station and made our way to The Albion pub in the old town, some way down the hill from The Winter Gardens, hoping to make a couple of pints before last orders, which in 1981, were still at the ridiculous time of 2.30pm.

Although I soon noticed there were no other mods around, this wasn't unusual as it was a mid-week gig and consequently, there was no real reason for people to turn up before the doors opened at 7pm. We knew the sound-check was scheduled later on so thought we'd take a leisurely stroll up the hill to the venue at about three-ish. A few pints were quickly put away and we stopped to grab a take away from a fish and chip shop on the sea front. And this is where we realised all was not well.

As you walk up the sea front hill in Margate there is an old Rocker's pub called The Britannia (which is still there and still patronised by Rockers to this day). We weren't worried about it because, past closing time, it would have been empty – instead, lounging around in the car park were a small gang of skinheads. There's weren't enough to worry us, maybe six or seven but they did shout some abuse as we walked past. We ignored them. Steve Roadrunner was hoping to cram in a quick interview before the sound-check so we put our heads down and carried on up the hill. It was only when we were about 40 yards from the doors of The Winter Gardens that I looked back and saw that their number had doubled or even trebled and that they were running up the hill carrying bricks, which they threw at us. Fortunately, no one was hit and we banged on the stage doors which were immediately opened and we gratefully stumbled in.

The skinheads soon disappeared and we assumed that would be the end of it.

But it wasn't, it was the beginning.

Steve Roadrunner had sat down with the bass player, the impeccably dressed Mark Ellis and started the interview when they were soon joined by drummer, Paul Wincer. I'd featured the band in a recent issue so wasn't taking too much notice of proceedings and instead made my way outside to have a look at the sea. I wished I hadn't as the number of skinheads had grown exponentially – this time there were around 50 of them and as soon as they saw me, they started jeering and cat calling and suddenly chased me as a group. I pegged it back to the stage door and just managed slam it shut behind me when they started banging on it.

There were only a handful of mods inside the cavernous venue and when the small windows of the Gents toilets were smashed in with a brick I started to worry about the gig. The band, on stage and performing their sound-check were unaware of the growing situation.

As the clocks hit half five, the pubs opened their doors and we decided to risk a trip to the Rose In June, a quiet boozer about two hundred yards away but hidden behind the Police Station just off Trinity Square.

I assumed the rain would have driven the skins away – there is nothing more depressing than a British seaside town in the middle of winter – but unfortunately it had become a light drizzle and wasn't enough to deter the glue-sniffers from further trouble.

We got back to the Winter Gardens unscathed but could see hundreds of green bomber jackets spreading out at the bottom of the hill, effectively cutting off the venue from the station.

The doors opened at seven and I was underwhelmed by the lack of rush. The band had been playing to pretty much sold out venues, but it was obvious that Margate wasn't going to rank among their most popular gigs. It soon became apparent why.

A few early arrivals who'd driven to the venue told of a number of skinhead gangs rampaging and marauding through the town, setting on any unsuspecting mods as they got off the train or bus. Several arrived battered and bloody and told of many more fleeing Margate completely, abandoning the gig.

The rest of the night rushed past in a blur. I remember nothing of the unremarkable support band and the cavernous venue was barely a quarter full as the foursome took to the stage. In those dark and distant days concert halls like The Winter Gardens had their security provided by a group of retired ex-servicemen called The Corps of Commissionaires. They wore a black uniform with a white plasticized Sam Brown cross belt and often sported their medal ribbons. There was rarely trouble and the concept of bouncers didn't exist like it does today.

Soon the skinheads tried rushing the doors and obviously the three old chaps were no match for them. But surprisingly they managed to hold on and, joined with half a dozen mods barricaded the glass front doors with a table. Inevitably a chair was put through them and the Police turned up, took one look at the situation and scarpered, waiting for reinforcements. They didn't have far to come as the Police Station is only thirty yards from the venue and within ten minutes the entire West Kent Constabulary – or rather, the ones that were on duty – had pitched up and steamed into the skins with truncheons drawn.

This distraction provided a window and although the band were still playing, a couple of dozen young mods made a break for it. We stayed till the end though, after all, we'd come a long way to see our band and regardless of what the boneheads were doing, wanted to see the encore.

The Lambrettas shuffled off stage to somewhat muted applause but had managed to cope with a strange situation very well. Skinheads smashing up gigs was a relatively regular occurrence in the early 80's but this was different. Word had been passed around their 'community' to head to Margate and 'crack some mod heads', well they took over the whole town; a bunch of rabid, shaven headed morons with bleached Levi's and 20 hole DM's with an average age of around 23 managed to terrify and beat up a bunch of skinny 16 year olds. Well done lads!

We blagged a lift to the station in a Police van and although the gangs had pretty much dispersed, I didn't really want to take any chances! The last train to London chugged into Kings Cross at about half twelve and our memorable trip to Margate was over!

Amanda: I caught up with Steve James on the phone in July 2020. He said…

Steve James: I worked at Parkgate Studios a fair bit during the early eighties, producing Toyah's album 'The Blue Meaning' there in 1980. I went on to work with The Lambrettas at Parkgate at the beginning of 1981. As I remember I set them up in the studio as though it was a live performance. Parkgate had a massive recording room, and so I got them playing together as much as I could to produce a more "live" sound, with not so much layering. Their drummer left after only a week and so I suggested they use Steve Bray, Toyah's drummer, as I had only recently worked with him. Steve Bray stayed with them to finish the recording but they got themselves another drummer for live gigs. I remember them being lovely guys and maybe a bit naughty! I always had a great time at Parkgate, and their wives made and brought me over a birthday cake!

Steve James went on to work with Paul Young, Kiki Dee, The Rutles and the Teletubbies among other things and now lives with his family in Australia.

Ike: Rocket were looking to follow up on the band's initial success with a second album. They needed to find the right kind of producer. A few months prior to this I had worked with a then very young Toyah Wilcox on her first album 'The Blue Meaning', which had been cut and mixed at Parkgate. Her producer was Steve James, son of the famed British actor of 'Carry On' fame. Coincidentally my father had been a very famous racetrack gambler and knew Sid, as Sid liked more than the occasional 'flutter'. I liked Steve's approach, he was very much a 'vibe' producer, and liked to get into the guts of what a band was all about, rather than approaching everything with a clean pop chart sound, which, clever as that can be, was not where the band wanted to go for the rest of their careers. They were a powerhouse live, and wanted to reproduce that on an album. Steve was the perfect fit for them. I had to convince Sally Atkins, head of Rocket Records' A&R team. She took a bit of convincing, and I got the impression the label wanted more music like 'Poison Ivy'. However, she agreed. I also had to meet with John Reid, then Elton John's business partner and his manager. We had the meeting in Reid's office. It was the stuff of 1980's rock and roll extravaganza. A white carpet that if it had been a lawn would have needed mowing, covered the floor. The centrepiece was a coffee table made from two Rolls Royce radiator grills with a glass top set between them. Reid was wearing mascara, which seemed at odds with his heavy Scottish accent. He was a powerful character and I felt more than a little intimidated during the meeting. Anyway, he seemed supportive of what the band wanted to achieve so all was well. Steve set the band up in the studio almost as if they were playing live on a stage. A technique that always worked for live working bands like them. Studios are intimidating places for a lot of musicians who only go into them to make a record. To people like me and Steve who had spent most of our working lives in them they were like home. Steve got a great sound, live, punchy and gritty round the edges. The main recording room was huge with a high ceiling, and Steve made the best use of it; lots of ambient microphones as well as close mics. They were able to lay down the tracks in the 'old school' way, playing as a tight cohesive unit and as us engineers say "recording air moving". Sadly with a few exceptions it is now a lost art. Most records today are made on computers, piece by piece with every track laid down separately. The album sounded great. I recall it as one of the best sessions we turned out at Parkgate, and we turned out a lot. Deff Leppard, McCartney, Paul Young, Simple Minds, Gerry Rafferty, Roger Daltrey.

As Ike was their manager and owned Parkgate Studios, they spent a lot of time there. It was only 25 miles from home, but because it was residential, they sometimes stayed over.

While recording 'Ambience', they released a couple of singles: 'Good Times' on 6th March 1981 and 'Anything You Want' on 24th April 1981.

Jez & Doug outside Parkgate

Paul McCartney and Wings were booked into Parkgate for April, so The Lambrettas finished up in March to make room for them. Steve Bray stayed to record Ambience, but then he left on 18th March, and Patrick Freyne joined. Patrick had been friends with Doug since they were 5 years old at nursery school, and they had often played in bands together both prior to, and after, The Lambrettas.

Doug: When we were gigging, we had a lorry with our PA, lights and backline driven around by our Roadie and soundmen & lighting fella, etc. We had thought this was quite impressive. When Paul McCartney's stuff arrived, we were swiftly put in our place with his 4 x Edwin Shirley trucks on permanent hire. One of his staff loaded in his guitars, about 40-50 of them. When things went quiet, we had a look at some of them. Mark found the Hofner violin bass. We opened the case and on the top of it was a set list covered in yellowed Sellotape. It was only about 10 songs, a couple of covers and shortened versions of the songs such as 'Tripper'. Lesser men might have thought it a good souvenir, but we were just in awe, particularly Mark. Obviously, we got to have a sneaky twang. The set list story has

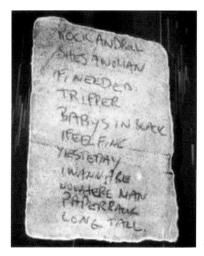

Paul McCartney's set list from his Hofner violin bass

been regaled on numerous occasions by all of us who saw it. Only very recently we found out that it has its own story if you google it! So, after all these years we were able to see a photo of what we saw on his guitar.

Amanda: Paul McCartney and Wings were in the studio after The Lambrettas. One of the girls who worked at Parkgate used to go to a local greengrocer's shop, and she was friendly with the lady who worked there. Linda McCartney went with her one day to buy some fruit, and the greengrocer asked who they had in the studio? Linda answered *"No-one very interesting at the moment"*. I wonder if the greengrocer ever realised who she was talking to?

Ambience was released in May 1981.

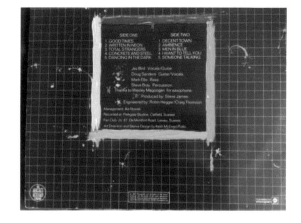

Patrick: It was great to join in March 1981. Ike was the manager at the time and as I remember it, the early days involved visits to his studio in Catsfield where the finishing touches were being put on 'Ambience', a couple of Rocket Records meetings with Sally Atkins and Co. at the Lancaster Gate HQ, and also rehearsals at the by then more or less derelict Cinema in Seaford. One of the early priorities was getting a new kit: sadly my old Hayman kit had been stolen from a very dodgy rehearsal space some time before and while I'd been able to afford a relatively cheap Premier Olympic kit with a cymbal and a hi-hat to 'tide me over' I needed a new one and Jez seemingly felt that since Rocket hadn't made many recent investments, we might be able get them to foot the bill, so off went Jez and I for a meeting with John Hall, who, after being initially pretty sceptical (something along the lines of "*How have you managed to get a drummer with no kit!?*") conceded and so Jez and I then went off to Drum City in Portobello Road to buy some drums.

The band had to rehearse-in Patrick during April, straight after they finished recording. His first gig was at Millfield School in Somerset on 9th May 1981. Whether at a tiny venue or a posh private school, dressing rooms are the same the world over!

Dressing Room Millfield School: Jez, Fiona, Mark

Dressing Room Millfield School: Amanda

Millfield School gig

Patrick: The night before the first gig, Jez and I returned from one of several short sort of PR trips. It could have been Edinburgh; we flew up there for some reason? Also, Radio One (I've still got the pen somewhere), Rotherham and Coventry, set up to meet fans and do radio interviews (during which, fortunately, Jez did most of the talking). I drove to Somerset the next day with amongst others, Mark plus the new drum kit in my parents' old blue van. I really enjoyed that first gig.

The day after Patrick's first gig was a charity football match at the Chelsea ground on Sunday 10th May. They all caught the train up to Stamford Bridge from Lewes. Each band who was there had a team, and they were all allowed one professional footballer. The Lambrettas professional was Stan Bowles, who I think mostly played for Manchester City. They beat the first team they played, Cosy Powell's All Stars. In the next round they were up against

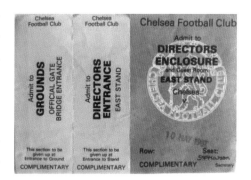

Charity Football ticket

The Baron Knights, who beat them. Elton John was in the stands with Jimmy Hill, the football pundit. He was a little disappointed his protegees didn't progress any further

in the competition, and especially that they were beaten by The Baron Knights!

Doug: My son Ben was about 6 and he went over and chatted with Elton and Jimmy Hill. When he came back, we asked him what they were talking about; he replied "*Don't know, they didn't recognise me!*" They hadn't met him before, so obviously didn't recognise him!

There were not so many gigs during 1981 and 1982, but one that seems to be fondly remembered was The Rainbow in Finsbury Park on 1st August.

RIGHT, BELOW
LEFT AND RIGHT:
Rainbow All Dayer

RIGHT: *Rainbow All Dayer:*

Anyone recognise their younger selves?

On 7th August 1981, their 7th single, 'Decent Town' was released. This was released as a 7" single with a live version of 'D-a-a-ance' on the B side. It was also released as a 12" with 'Decent Town' and 'Total Strangers' on the A side, and 2 live tracks on the B side.

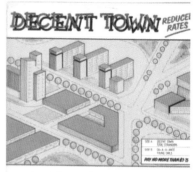

Over the next few months, they played in Spain and Holland, along with a few British gigs, however sadly things were beginning to die down a bit. They also spent time visiting and recording some radio shows, and they had some more publicity photos done.

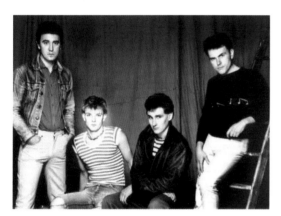

The gigs in Spain were on 29th, 30th and 31st October. Derek Haggar had gone off to do some Roadie work for David Essex at this point, so they took a friend of Jez's; Kevin Stagg to drive and Roadie for them, both in Spain and Holland.

Although previous to working with The Lambrettas Derek had a completely different career, afterwards he stayed in the music industry. He worked with David Essex, John Watts, A-Ha and Cliff Richard, among others. He still works as a Stage Manager to this day, always for Cliff Richard, but sometimes for other artists as well.

> **Patrick**: We flew out of Gatwick, but the plane was somewhat delayed and so we were very late for the first night. Mark and I were sitting together on the plane and neither of us liked flying, but when the fuselage started inexplicably filling up with smoke midway through the journey, Mark seemed to be the calmest of everyone, telling us "*I told*

you we were going to die!".We were met by a guy called Miguel, who owned the club, and as our flight had been delayed, he drove us straight to the venue. That first night, the equipment that Miguel had hired in for us was not very good at all, in fact I remember the hi-hat

moved around on its axis, and I had to hold it with my left hand to keep it standing! The following two nights were so much better. We had managed to get Miguel to acquire some half-decent equipment and the second night the club was full to bursting. I had already played good gigs with the band and of course, amateur and semi-pro gigs before, that were attended by fairly approving and enthusiastic audiences, but this was something else; the crowd went bananas and when that happens, as I'm sure the rest of band already knew from experience, it boosts your confidence, you play better and get into a sort of feedback loop with the audience (the more you put into your playing, the more they like it and so you put even more into your playing, etc.).

We went to Holland twice, in short succession around the end of 1981/beginning of 1982 and on at least one of the trips, we took the boat out of Harwich to the Hook of Holland (nine or ten hours at sea) and needed to fill out a carnet because we took our own equipment and Kevin Stagg also came along as roadie.

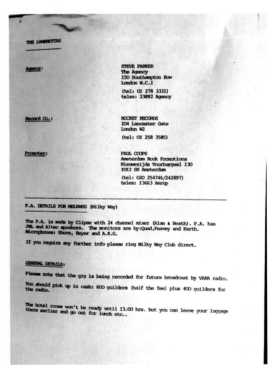

Itinerary

We seemed to have quite a few visitors when we were on the 3-day trip in January 1982. From Rocket there was John Hall, Robert Key (nice guy with a good sense of humour) and Sally Atkins. Peter Haines was also visiting Amsterdam and met us in the hotel. I think that was about the only time I met him and he seemed like a good enough bloke.

Sally Atkins: The gigs got better and better, I loved seeing them live, they had great songs and an incredible energy.

Sally Atkins in Holland

Towards the end of 1981 Ike decided he wanted to concentrate more on his studio. He had never managed a band before and had worked with the Lambrettas just over a year. Although he enjoyed the time, the studio was really more "his thing", especially as at that time he had Paul McCartney in most of the time.

Ray Santilli became The Lambrettas final manager, and stayed with them through to the end of the band in that era. After The Lambrettas, Ray went on to all sorts; as a musician and record and film producer. He is probably best known for his exploitation in 1995 of the controversial 'alien autopsy' footage. In 2006 Warner Brothers made a film about this, with Ant and Dec taking the main parts. Dec played Ray and Ant played his business partner Gary Shoefield. The Lambrettas have had so many different eccentric, weird and wonderful characters involved with them over the years, and have had some good fun times with all of them!

A couple of London gigs came after Amsterdam, and then in April Doug and Jez went to do a charity radio quiz in London.

Doug: I remember Mike Read being the quiz master. I also remember Kim Wilde being

the HMV Shop sponsor longest ever radio music
quiz for Nordoff-Robbins Music Therapy Centre

The HMV Shop chain is to sponsor a music quiz - lasting the marathon time of 26 hours 385 minutes - in aid of the Nordoff-Robbins Music Therapy Centre this coming Easter weekend. The event is to be broadcast extensively by Radio 1 and will be organised by the research company MRIB.

The quiz - at the Collegiate Theatre in Gordon Street, Euston - will run from 9.55am on Good Friday, April 9th through till 6.25pm on Easter Saturday, April 10th between a Music Industry team and Radio 1. The question master will be Mike Read, with Paul Gambaccini captaining the Radio 1 team and the broadcast commentary by David Jensen and Steve Wright.

Anyone involved with the music business or Radio 1 is invited to pit his or her wits be it for five minutes or five hours. Record buyers and Radio 1 listeners will also be represented on the two teams.

Radio 1 will be broadcasting from the theatre every hour throughout the quiz, including a five hour stint from midnight. Radio production will be handled by Trevor Dann, Stuart Grundy and Johnny Beerling. The entire event is being organised by MRIB'S Dafydd Rees, who conceived the idea and should be contacted by any interested parties.

Further details of the quiz will be available throughout the HMV Shop chain. at the end of February, and fund-raising proposals in subsequent press releases. All the money raised from the quiz will be donated to the Music Therapy Charity.

There are more than 64,000 handicapped children in the United Kingdom. In recent years music has been used with clinical direction to help those suffering from severe disabilities. The work of Dr.Paul Nordoff has had a very specific and far reaching influence in this field. In 1959 he met Dr. Clive Robbins, a teacher of handicapped children, at Sunfield Children's Home in Worcestershire and there began their work together which lasted until Dr.Nordoff's death in 1977. Without the support of the Music Therapy Charity, the work of Nordoff and Robbins would never have progressed. After several years of intensive fund raising, the Nordoff-Robbins Music Therapy Centre is now firmly established.

Help this charity in contributing to the quiz by taking part be you a broadcaster, journalist, producer, songwriter, publisher, A&R manager, press officer, promotion man, marketing manager or even record company executive - and especially if you are a recording artist.

for further information : Dafydd Rees (01) 408 0250/629 1172

Tony Brainsby (Publicity) (01) 834 8341

They have specifically asked for the Lambrettas.

Music quiz flyer

there; not sure if she was on our team or another one. I answered quite a few questions, and I don't know why, but I can remember one of them was "*Who sang walking back to happiness?*" I knew it was Helen Shapiro! No-one else did. At the end of our session of the quiz, Jez was in one of his hyper moods and he grabbed an acoustic guitar. He played, and we both sang 'My Old Man's a Dustman'. We found out after that they had recorded it and over the next week or so they kept playing it on Radio 1. It actually didn't sound too bad at all.

At the beginning of 1982 The Lambrettas went back to their roots, rehearsing at the Scout Hut in Lewes where they had started. They decided to release another cover, and Mark suggested 'Somebody to Love', which was a 1967 hit for the psychedelic rock band, Jefferson Airplane. They asked Peter Collins back to produce it, put 'Nobody's Watching Me' on the B-side, and it was released on 26th February 1982. 'Nobody's Watching Me' was written by the four of them and produced by them as well. They recorded these songs at a place called Southern Studios in Wood Green, and they were engineered by John Loder and Simaen Skolfield. This was their 8th single, and proved to be their last.

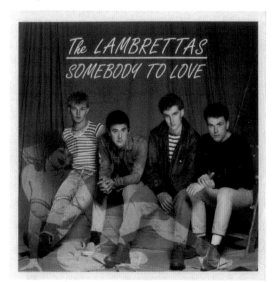

Somebody to Love cover

No-one really knows why, but they re-pressed it in April with 'Leap Before You Look' on the B-side, and coincided this release with a big showcase gig at The Venue in Victoria on 14th April. They added brass and backing singers, and the show was almost sold out. Paul Wincer turned up backstage, and any ill feelings from the previous year were mended. Derek Haggar was also back with them for this gig. This turned out to be The Lambrettas last gig in that era, so they went out on a high. It was also the last

The Venue gig

time that any more than 2 of the original band played together! Mark moved back to Los Angeles on 13th January 1983, and he sometimes came back to visit family, but didn't very often catch up with the others in the band, although Doug and he met up a couple of the first few times he returned.

Mark: There were European tours, TOTP appearances, meeting celebrities, etc., but for me the highlight of my time in The Lambs was going on TISWAS, and meeting Spit the Dog backstage, then being hit by the Phantom Flan Flinger on live TV! To this day, I still have never seen a tape of the show. Despite some ups and downs, being in

Doug with Mark
before he left for the States

The Lambs was the best time of my life. Even that short-lived small amount of success was very seductive. Nothing has compared since.

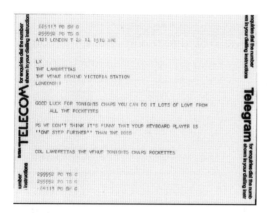

Venue telegram

Venue ticket

Patrick: I did enjoy the (what turned out to be our 'final') gig at the Venue; I seem to remember that on or about the day we got a 'good wishes' telegram from Rocket. Some old faces turned up, and in that sense, it turned out, by chance, to be a sort of celebration. However, I think by that time the band had become too 'dilute' in terms of image, marketing, etc. I think that if I learned anything about the music business at that time, it was perhaps that A&R needed to be able to see a clear and obvious route to financial return and so that meant that if a band was going to be commercially successful, it had to have an equally clear, firm and obvious proposition in terms of music and image. The original Lambrettas had that: great, catchy songs, a smart image and an identifiable following, record buying public – A

Patrick and Doug

complete package and so in that sense the drum chair really always belonged to Paul. The music business is just that; a business! One thing I can say for sure, once you've had (as in my case) even a 'taster' of life as a professional pop (nothing wrong with pop!) musician, the 'nine to five' is a VERY poor substitute, indeed.

64

PART TWO – THE NINETIES

This period was a bit spread out and a lasting reunion was never really the aim.

In 1992, Jez contacted Doug and asked him if he would join him in doing a couple of Lambrettas gigs. He reckoned that the time might be right to get people interested again. As Mark had already moved to Los Angeles, he asked Dave Purdye to play bass. (Dave had played in a previous incarnation of Shakedown with Doug, before Jez had joined, and had also played with John Watts of Fischer Z.) Also joining them was Jez's brother-in-law Duncan Muir on keyboards, and a drummer called James Newman, who was a friend of Jez.

> **Dave Purdye**: I'd played with Doug and Jez for a while during the eighties after the original Lambrettas had disbanded in a band called Rave On Jack. Jez called me up one day out of the blue and said that he and Doug were going to get the Lambrettas back together. He explained that Mark was living in the States and asked me if I'd be interested in playing bass with them. I agreed and I think we did about a dozen gigs in total, including some London dates and the Brighton Centre. As everyone knows, The Lambrettas have got some great songs and arrangements, and Mark's bass lines are second to none. So, it was a really good experience and one I'm glad I had the opportunity to do.

The first gig they played was at The George Robey in London on 22 August 1992. London based band The Direction played with The Lambrettas at this first gig at the Robey. They also played together at the Powerhaus in December of that year. The Direction were together from 1991 until 1995, they had a few line-up changes over those four years, but in 1992 Tim Groves was on drums.

The George Robey, L-R: Doug, Jez, Dave Purdye

George Robey Ticket

Tim Groves (from The Direction): The Direction first supported The Lambrettas at the George Robey. I have no recollection of us playing, but made sure I hung around to see their set, I was always more of a Beat Boy than Glory Boy, they were fantastic. Next, I heard we were supporting them at the Powerhaus (as part of a mini tour). I recall being told by Paul Seipel that we were going to cover 'My Side of Heaven' by Back to Zero. This song never made it to Medway, I had never heard it before and here I was about to play it with Brian Kotz singing, in front of a packed Powerhaus, I was shitting

myself! We played the gig, The Lambrettas were superb again. After, back stage, I plucked up courage to ask Jez Bird for an autograph, he refused... but instead asked me for mine!! My Mod Revival life was complete!! My main memory was of Jez being an incredibly friendly, humble and generous person. I wish I could thank him now; he made a crap drummer in an average band feel very very special.

Tim Groves from The Direction

The Lambrettas played a few more gigs around London in late 1992 and 1993. Jez organised another coach trip from Lewes for a second date at The Robey. The last gig

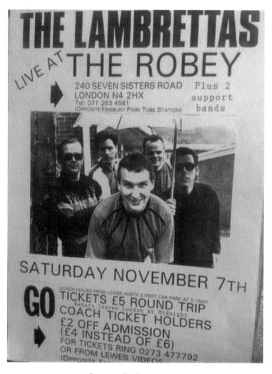

George Robey poster

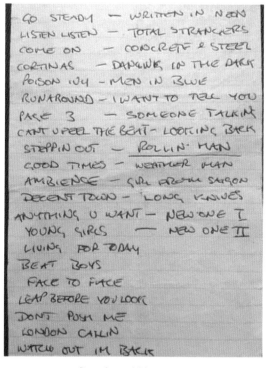

Doug's scribbles: songs

REMEMBER the singles Poison Ivy, D-a-a-ance and Page Three? Then you must have been a fan of early Eighties Brighton mod outfit **The Lambrettas**. From their early gigs at the now demolished Alhambra pub on Brighton seafront, to signing a record deal with Elton John's Rocket label to touring Europe with Madness, The Lambrettas were very much a part of the mod revival that saw Two Tone, parkas and the film Quadrophenia placed firmly in the public eye. But an unlucky break saw them miss out on a tour of the U.S. with Ultravox and the band finally split in 1982 after covering the Jefferson Airplane song Somebody To Love. Now though they have reformed and tomorrow night you can catch Jez Bird and his mates running through all the old numbers, and a few new ones, at the Brighton Centre East Wing at 8.30pm.

was at Brighton Centre on 5th June 1993. They then took another break and went back to their own ventures. Jez playing his one man shows, and Doug playing with his band The Poor Brave Things.

Paul Macnamara (Mac): My love for The Lambrettas can be traced back to the Summer of 1980.

My older brother had just seen the band play at The Top Rank in Cardiff and on arrival home from the gig threw me a 'Beat Boys In The Jet Age' tour badge along with a drum stick he had acquired courtesy of drummer Paul Wincer.

I quickly went about collecting the band's records and joined the fan club, which was expertly run by Jo (Amanda). Although I was in my early teens and too young to catch the band live, I followed their career with great interest. 'Beat Boys' remains one of my favourite albums of all time and 'Ambience', although taking the band in a different direction still had its moments.

The mod revival had seen its day by 1982, and although the band's split came as no surprise, I was still disappointed, and sent a letter to the fan club asking the band to reconsider.

Fast forward to 1992 and again I can thank my brother for finally giving me the opportunity to see the Lambrettas live. He had just returned from London after seeing Madness at the Madstock event at Finsbury Park. We discussed the gig, and I said, shame it wasn't The Lambrettas. He said; well they are playing a reunion gig at The George Robey soon. I didn't believe him but he said there are loads of posters around London, it's true.

So, it was August 1992 when me and two pals made the trip from Cardiff and finally got to see the band play. Jez and Doug, supported by new recruits brought the house down with an electric set. The reunion was quite short lived, but I also managed to see them again at The Powerhaus.

With the tragic passing of Jez, I thought that was it, but thanks to Doug and Paul bringing the band back together again in 2009, I have been lucky enough to see them play again at least another 30 times.

My wife and I always look forward to seeing the band play and have struck up a great friendship with all those involved with the band, including original bass player Mark Ellis, who despite now living in the States, still keeps in touch regularly.

L-R: *Michelle Macnamara, Doug, Chris Venzi-James, Paul Macnamara, Paul, Phil Edwards; 2012*

Listen, Listen, Listen. The Lambrettas rock.

Amanda: We searched all through our fan club memorabilia, but sadly we couldn't find Mac's letter asking them not to split. However, we did find this card sent to Doug back in the day! How innocent were those times?!

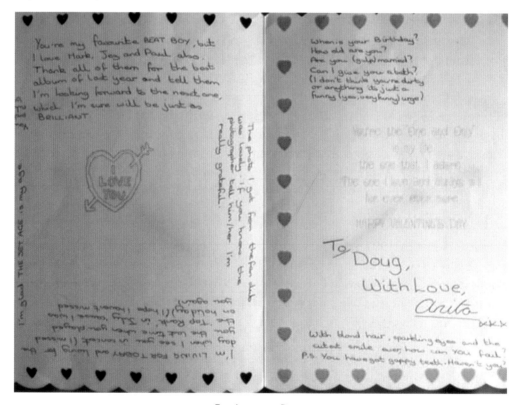

Fan Letter to Doug

The Lambrettas used Nigel Lavender as a Roadie, both for the gigs in 1992-93, and also the ones they did in 1995. Nigel was the brother of Ian Lavender, who was a friend and occasionally did a bit of stage security for The Lambrettas back in the eighties. Nigel was friends with Doug and also played with him in The Poor Brave Things.

Nigel Lavender: I travelled around with The Lambrettas to help out a bit during the nineties. We did a few gigs round London, Kent and Brighton in 1992-93, a couple of times at the George Robey, which were great gigs, pretty packed! We had a bit of a break, and then a few more in 1995. In between those times, Doug had discovered pyro-technics after doing some stage work at Glyndebourne Opera House just down the road from us. So, he had acquired a small pyro-flash system including two pod

holders, and located a shop in Brighton that sold the actual pyro-flash cartridges! Health & Safety at indoor venues these days would never allow this, but we used them at most of the 1995 gigs, and I don't recall asking permission, just setting them off. Anyway, the first gig was at Lewes Town Hall, two days after Bonfire Night. Doug's brother Donald was there to help me, as I was guitar teching as well as being in charge of these pyros! I had the device with the button and Donald was running round the stage re-filling the pods with the cartridges. We set fire to a backdrop at the back of the stage behind Patrick's kit! It was ok as we managed to put it out really quickly, but we still carried on using them until the end of the night.

Nigel Lavender

In 1995, Jez contacted Doug again and they decided to do a few more shows. This time they asked Patrick Freyne to come back to play drums, and Duncan moved over to play bass.

On Thursday 30 March 1995, they appeared on the Channel 4 early morning show The Big Breakfast, with Mark Little and Dani Behr. They played 'D-a-a-ance' and then played out the programme with 'Poison Ivy'.

THE **BIG** BREAKFAST

MEAL VOUCHER

THIS VOUCHER ENTITLES YOU TO ONE
FREE BREAKFAST

The Big Breakfast: Dani Behr and Jez

The Big Breakfast: Doug

The Big Breakfast: Patrick

The Big Breakfast: Duncan Muir

The Big Breakfast

70

Patrick: When we did the Big Breakfast I noticed, just before broadcasting, that someone had taped a sign in my bass drum saying something like "*Paula, Paula so sweet and so twee, please Michael Hutchence give her one for me*", which I got rid of quickly (because I didn't want to be part of that bit of scandal) – you may remember that the BB was produced by Planet 24, the production company co-owned by Bob Geldof!

The Big Breakfast

After the Big Breakfast, there were a few more gigs towards the end of 1995; Lewes Town Hall, Bradford, Dublin Castle and finally, Nottingham on Saturday 9 December 1995.

Doug: I remember that last Nottingham gig we drove home from it in Jez's van. We dropped Patrick off at his car where we had collected him before the gig. He lived in Kennington, and had driven to, and parked just off the M25! It was really late (or really early morning!) and snowing, and the van wasn't running properly. As Jez came to drop me off, the van couldn't get up the hill to where I lived, so I had to ring Amanda to get up at about 7am and come and get me and my equipment in our car.

This was the last time that Doug and Jez played a live Lambrettas gig together, although a couple of times in the early noughties Doug just turned up at Jez's one man shows to sing a few songs with him!

PART THREE 2009 TO DATE

his part has to start with the sadness from the previous year. In August 2008, Jez sadly passed away after fighting a battle with cancer. Doug, Ben, Paul, Peter Haines, Derek Haggar and myself were among a large number of people who attended his funeral to say goodbye and to show support to Fiona, their two sons, Henry and Charlie and his mother, Eileen. Mark sent his best wishes to Fiona, but unfortunately wasn't able to return from America in time to attend the funeral.

I thought I would choose a nice photo of Jez from back then to put in here. And Jez, if you're watching, I hope you're pleased that some of those words you wrote 40 years ago are still being sung to people today. I know your family and friends are all very proud of you.

Dave Wyburn: The late 70s was a fantastic time to be growing up with music! Music was always being played in my parent's house, but I took my influence from my older cousin. He told me "Mod is coming back". Anyway, on one fateful night in 1980 he had offered me to tag along to a gig in Swindon at the Brunel Rooms. I had to keep quiet about my age, but it would be fun! The band playing were The Lambrettas. I had already heard a few of their catchy tunes, so off we went. Not sure of the date but I know it was a weekend as I didn't have school the next day! We got to the gig and it really was buzzing; parkas, suits and Union Jacks and scooters everywhere. The gig started; it was my first experience of a gig. It was very cramped and felt quite intimidating. I couldn't see much but Mike and Phil hoisted me up in the air to see more. The Lambrettas started their set and it all went mental! I'm sure they played a few 60s covers but over the years my memory has faded slightly. 'Poison Ivy' and 'Go Steady' were the catalyst. The stage was quite low but I managed to get a glimpse of The Lambrettas on stage in their suits, Jez bounced around like Zebedee on speed and had a great stage presence. I remember Doug and Jez sharing the mic a few times. I was exhausted at the end of the gig, covered in sweat from dancing. I finally admitted I

Dave Wyburn

was a mod! After the revival faded, the influence, style and music has always stayed with me, and I share my memories and experiences with my children and they too even know a few lyrics to 'Poison Ivy'. Sadly, I heard of Jez's death in 2008, and to me these guys were my mates, talking to me through the music, so to say. I went to the funeral in Lewes on my newly acquired scooter, firstly meeting Jez's wife Fiona, and their sons. Then, after the funeral I met the rest of the band and their families; Doug, Amanda, Paul etc. They were all ace! I have one thing to say to you guys; Jez, Fiona, Amanda, Doug, Paul, Mark and Peter – a massive thank you. My legs still ache.

Dave Wyburn, The Beat Boy.

In 2009 a guy called Dave Wyburn, who was a mod that we met at Jez's funeral rang me up. He said he was putting on an event to celebrate 30 years of the film Quadrophenia, and he asked if Doug and Paul would do a short Lambrettas set at the event. At first, they weren't sure at all, but Dave was quite persuasive, so they said they'd give it a go! At the time Doug was playing with a local band called Zen House, and Paul was running his drum shop in Dorset.

Paul: Really, to be absolutely honest, the reforming of anything Lambrettas was not something I ever wanted to do, feeling it was better left alone. However, it was nice to catch up with Doug in 2008 after not seeing each other for about 20 years. Obviously, the reason for catching up was not the best, as it was for Jez's funeral. I had moved down to Poole and opened my drum shop, Poole Percussion in the late eighties. Doug and I were really not sure about this gig, but we chewed it over and decided it would be a nice idea.

Poole Percussion was actually one of the most renowned drum shops in the country, and until 2012 was leading the way in the drum and percussion industry. It was housed in a warehouse on an industrial estate. They had massive stocks and used to run drum clinics with artists such as; Terry Bozzio, Dennis Chambers, Carl Palmer, Billy Cobham, Gregg Bissonette, Ian Paice, Steve White and Chad Smith. Notably Chad Smith bought

One side of the Poole Percussion warehouse

Steve White a drum kit one Christmas from Poole Percussion.

Paul and Doug discussed how to go about things and decided the only way to do it would be for Doug to move over from playing a lot of guitar and some vocals, to doing a lot of vocals and some guitar. They were joined by Phil Edwards on guitar and

Chris Venzi-James on bass, who both came from Poole. So, Doug travelled down to Poole for a few weekends to rehearse with the 3 of them. They chose 16 songs for their set.

Phil: When Paul asked Chris and I to join him and Doug to do a Lambrettas reunion gig in 2009, I was up for it straight away as it sounded like a great opportunity. Doug and Amanda came down to meet us and it was agreed we would do some rehearsals at Paul's drum shop.

1.	FACE TO FACE
2.	CAN'T YOU FEEL THE BEAT
3.	GO STEADY
4.	DECENT TOWN
5.	HARD TO HANDLE
6.	DANCE
7.	LIVING FOR TODAY
8.	PAGE THREE
9.	LISTEN LISTEN
10.	LEAP BEFORE YOU LOOK
11.	CORTINAS
12.	LONDON CALLING
13.	RUNAROUND
14.	GRAPEVINE
15.	BEAT BOYS IN THE JET AGE
16.	POISON IVY

Brighton Concorde 2 set list

LEFT: *Rehearsals 2009*

Dave Wyburn had to pull out of the event at the last minute, but his partner Jenny Bignell took over organising everything. Peter Haines had turned up again at this point and he acted on our behalf for this event.

ABOVE: *Amanda and Peter Haines*

LEFT: *Brighton flyer*

Jenny Bignell: 2009, 30 years of the iconic 'Mod' film; Quadrophenia, an idea was born to celebrate the film. Together with two of my gig partners; Nelly Nelson and Debby Couzens, MODROPHENIA 79 was born, and Concorde 2 in Brighton was our chosen venue. Keeping the Mod and film theme, we opted for relevant musicians to play, and we were able to entice The Lambrettas to come out of retirement and headline the event for us, their first gig in over 25 years! With the actor, Gary Shail compering the event, The Hiwatts, Mark Joseph, and Timebomb joined The Lambrettas for a night of 'Mod'. The event was preceded by a ride out with mods on scooters to Beachy Head. I stayed at the venue during that time to welcome the musicians and to allay any concerns that members of The Lambrettas may have had after not gigging for so many

years. Dougie Sanders was by himself initially, looking a tad lost, but once we began chatting and the rest of the band arrived, their excitement was evident. Paul Wincer then informed me he had 30 guests on his guest list, all family, and why not! The evening was a great success all round. The Lambrettas were welcomed back with much enthusiasm and love; many memories were re-lived and many more were created for their fans. Most importantly, The Lambrettas decided to start touring and gigging again and now give much pleasure to their existing and ever-increasing fan base. *Thanks guys! Aunty Jen. X*

Jenny Bignell & Gary Shail

We turned up at the Concorde 2 in Brighton on 15th August 2009, not really knowing what to expect at all. At this stage they had no idea that people would want to come and see them, so all the original nerves were back again for Doug and Paul, while Phil and Chris didn't have a clue what to expect.

They hadn't had much time to prepare; it was the first time for 14 years that Doug had played the songs, and longer for Paul. They were, however, well received. After-

wards there were a lot of people there wanting things to be signed and to have photos taken with them.

Paul: It was mental. We didn't know anyone would still be interested! We met up with Gary Shail who we had known back in the day, but had not seen since then. We didn't realise that people were still following us and listening to our music.

Brighton 2009: Paul, Gary Shail, Doug

Phil: After the gig it was mayhem, it was

such an incredible night. The room was blasting with energy it was so exciting and everybody was on such a high! Afterwards, as it sunk in that it was all over, it was a bit of a come down, so we were really pleased when it looked like other people were interested in booking us. We all agreed we would carry on for the time being and to see how things would progress. I still find it amazing that 10 years later we're still doing it! We've been so lucky to play all over the UK and many countries around Europe – the passion that the fans have for the songs has made it all possible and it's been a real pleasure to perform them. It's why I always have a grin on my face when we're on stage.

We met some people at that first Brighton gig, and at subsequent ones, who are still friends today. This part was the biggest surprise and pleasure, both to me and Doug, as well as the rest of the band. Making friends with people who come to the gigs has been such a big part of the last 10 years for all of us.

Rob Wright: I first met The Lambrettas in 2009 at their reunion gig in Brighton, and I can say it was a fantastic experience. It took me back to when I was a teenager strutting my stuff on the dance floor to 'Poison Ivy', and one of my all-time favourites, 'D-a-a-ance'. I went to see them a few more times over the following few months and went down to Portsmouth the following summer. In September of 2010, when I brought them to do a gig in Runcorn, it was unbelievable. We've stayed in touch ever since, and catch up whenever we get a chance. It's great to class The Lambrettas, Amanda and Chez as good friends. I occasionally sell their merch for them and it's always a pleasure. *We've had some really funny times all over the country and especially in Dublin in 2011.*

Concorde 2 2009

After the Brighton gig the phone started ringing, so we decided to continue and see how it went. People were contacting Peter Haines, and although he had enjoyed the Brighton event, he didn't have time to take on managing the band. So, Doug and I went down to Poole. We met the other three in a farm shop café, and I agreed I would give it a go! It was a pretty steep learning curve! Being The Lambrettas manager these days means doing absolutely everything, both beforehand and on gig days. Back in the day, they had a Manager, Tour manager, 2 or 3 Roadies, a fan club person, secretaries, press officers, booking agents, accountants, etc. I had no idea in that farm shop café how busy I would be, as I do all of those things along with anything else that might come along!

There were a couple more gigs in 2009. The second one was at the 100 Club in London, and was arranged by Tony from Long Tall Shorty. They played with The Lambrettas that evening along with The Teenbeats, who we knew back in the '80s.

100 Club   *100 Club, Doug with Huggy Leaver*

Ben Sanders: I said to Dad that I didn't want to miss out this time round, as I was too young to go to the gigs first time! I went to the 100 Club in 2009, The Soundbar, Birmingham in January 2010, and a few more during 2010. At this stage I wasn't helping them as a Roadie.

Cheryl Shaw: The first time I met The Lambrettas was in April 2010. I had been in contact with the band as they were going to be playing the Isle of Wight Scooter Rally that summer and I was plugging them on my social media. I had seen Jez Bird play his one man show a few years earlier when I lived in Eastbourne. So anyway, Paul Wincer invited me to Southampton to meet them all and to watch a gig. I had no idea at that time that Paul and I would end up being a couple and that I would still be going to the gigs, and selling merchandise 10 years later!

Early on in 2010, we started to work with a Booking Agent called Mike Vine, and towards the end of that year we also started to work with Peter Barton from Rock

Artist Management (RAM). These days booking agents don't work exclusively with the smaller bands like The Lambrettas. They get us a date and arrange the fee, and then we usually organise all the housekeeping. We are still currently working with both Mike and RAM whenever they get us bookings.

Mike Vine: I had heard somewhere that The Lambrettas were playing Live again and as a fan of the band since I first heard 'Beat Boys in the Jet Age' when I was a teenager, I thought why not contact them and see if I could offer my agency services. I started booking live shows for the band in 2010 and arranged their 2010 Christmas tour. I have worked for them on and off ever since, and am

L-R: Phil Edwards, Paul, Mike Vine, Doug, Chris Venzi-James

happy to say the band are still on my roster, 10 years later. It has always been a pleasure working for and dealing with the band/management, and long may it continue.

Mostly when we work directly with promoters, they are as a 'one-off' event, but we have worked with some more than once. We started to work with Adrian Gibson from AGMP in 2011. AGMP are kind of in between our Booking Agents and the usual Promoters that we work with. They are a live music promotions company who work with the same venues and the same bands year on year.

One of the Promoters we worked with more than once was Sean Fletcher. Sean brought us over to play at Whelans in Dublin in February 2010. He got us back the following year to play at a Mod weekender event at a venue called The Village on Wexford Street, next to Whelans. We travelled over in a van on the overnight ferry

Backstage at Whelans, 2010

Whelans, 2010

Chris Venzi-James Waterford, 2011

from Wales to Rosslare. The ferry ride was so rough! There were six of us on that trip as we took Ben with us. The ferry was almost cancelled due to the rough weather. We all started off in the bar and ended up in the toilets! They played at The Forum in Waterford on 1st April 2011. The next day we drove up to Dublin and they were on the same night as From The Jam (FTJ). Sean always looks after his bands. He makes sure we get a comfortable hotel, food, drinks, etc., and is always checking we are ok. At this event, Sean used a guy called Andrew Gilbert as his stage manager. Andrew is a very good friend to all of us in The Lambrettas family, and we always look forward

The Village, Dublin, 2011

to meeting up with him. He used to come to gigs back in the '80s and his story is in part one. He mostly works with Secret Affair these days, but has helped us out on numerous occasions since 2011.

Ben: I went with them to Ireland for the weekend in April 2011. Me, Dad and Mum drove down to Phil's house in Poole where he had the van. We collected Paul and Chris and then drove to the ferry port in Wales. It was a night ferry, and when we first got on, we had a drink in the bar and it wasn't too rough. Once it left the harbour things got awful, everyone was trying to sleep but the ferry was rocking and banging up and down! Every time there was a bang, all the sleeping people sat up and looked around like a bunch of meerkats! Me, Paul and Mum were so sick! Waterford on the first night and was a good gig. The next night in Dublin was a great gig. Afterwards we spent time in the hotel bar with the FTJ blokes, Andy Gilbert and some other friends we met there who were in the same hotel. We had to catch a ferry back from Dublin the next day.

Dublin:
Amanda and Ben

Dublin:
Ben, Doug, Amanda

Dublin:
Doug, Bruce Foxton, Rob Wright

Paul and I had tried to book flights but we couldn't. However, it ended up not being so rough and a lot quicker than a few nights before, thank goodness. During that trip I was helping a bit with equipment, etc., and then later I started going with them more often as a Roadie, and began to learn what to do.

We worked with Sean again when he put on a show at the 229 Club, London in 2012.

Sean Fletcher, Modern Media: West of Ireland in the late 70s had one TV station, until RTE2 started broadcasting and we were opened up to the world of TOTP. The catchy theme tune was soon followed by a range of odd, strange diverse acts, but every now and then a gem appeared, one of those was The Lambrettas. Mod and cool, "Poison Ivy' has been covered by many acts but none as successful as the Lambrettas" said the suave BBC presenter. That was my first taste of the Lambrettas. With no recording facilities invented yet I had to wait 14 days more, and hope they climbed the chart to see them again! I managed two Thursday's later to connect our tv to our 70s Ferguson 20 D Music Centre. The Lambrettas rocked Society Street again and I soon realized there was more to them than just 'Poison Ivy'. 'D-a-a-ance' and 'Page 3' (purchased at huge expense in a Dublin cool record store) were to be played on the Ferguson 20 D for months.

Roll on the Modern Media years over 30 years later and I get a chance to work with the band as the promoter. Andy Warhol once said *"You should never meet your idols as you are setting yourself up for disappointment"*. I was very pleased to prove him wrong. Working with Doug, Paul and the band in Whelans Dublin for the band's first Irish gig in over 30 years was one of the most enjoyable gigs I have promoted. We had our very own stage invasion; a guy doing quite a 'Happy Dance' on stage left! Modfest followed the following year at The Village, Dublin, and The Lambrettas shone again. Modrophenia London in May 2012 was definitely the most difficult gig of my career! An Irish bloke putting on four UK Mod bands in London was a major challenge, but once again the Lambrettas made the whole weekend worth-while. A chat and a few drinks with

Amanda and Doug and their lovely crew, and I had all but forgotten about the comments from another act; "the stage is too small (for doing scissor kicks!)", plus I got the blame for the venue having a speaker in front of the stage. However, I am proud to say that Modrophenia London, difficult as it was, did treat the Lambrettas to luxurious accommodation, including bunk beds at the venue!

To walk on Brighton pier and see the well-deserved plaque to The Lambrettas is as important for Brighton as it is to the band.
I will always have great memories of the Lambrettas whether as a concert goer or promoter.

229 Flyer

Another Promoter we worked with more than once was Meurig Jones who booked us to play in one of our more unusual venues; Hercules Hall in Portmeirion on Friday 30th September 2011. This show took us to Portmeirion for a few days, which was a real treat. Paul, Cheryl, Doug and I travelled the 300 miles

Castell Deudraeth Hotel, Portmeirion

on the Thursday, and when we got there, we were pretty blown away by the amazing place we had arrived at. We stayed in the village, in a suite called The Arches. Meurig

The Arches Suite, Portmeirion

Portmeirion Tour:
Paul, Cheryl Shaw, Meurig Jones, ?, Doug

Portmeirion Buggy Tour

Portmeirion village

Portmeirion

took us out for a meal that evening to the Castell Deudraeth hotel which is at the entrance to the village. On the Friday morning, he took us on a tour of the village and the surrounding hills in a little buggy, and we discovered he has the most immense amount of knowledge about the place and the architect Clough Williams-Ellis, who was the creator of Portmeirion Village. Phil and Chris travelled up on the Friday, and they played the gig that night. We all left the following day. What a memorable few days! Oh, and they have the signed Lambrettas poster on the wall of fame in the Portmeirion office.

Meurig Jones: Having grown up in the 'best period of music' (in my opinion), the wonderful years of exciting music that was between 1977 and 1983, I absolutely loved the mod revival movement of 1979/80 in particular. I could identify more with that than any other musical 'tribe' of the time, with a passion.

I first became aware of the band when I heard 'Go Steady' on the radio, although my good friend was certain its title was 'Ghost Eddie'! I was glad to prove him wrong when

I bought the single at Corfields in Tywyn late '79. Then, wow! March 1980, 'Poison Ivy' was not only in the charts, but in the Top 10! Brilliant! For me, even better was to come, with the release of my favourite The Lambrettas track 'D-a-a-ance'! In this case it was released on a brilliantly striking picture disc, with its iconic photo of Brighton Pier! What was not to like about this wonderful release?!

If 'D-a-a-ance' was my song of the Spring of 1980, then 'Beat Boys in the Jet Age' was my album of the summer! I absolutely loved the LP and still do! A brilliant and vibrant collection of great tunes with iconic artwork, so perfect in every way!

My greatest regret of this era, was that as I lived in far off rural north Wales, it was practically impossible to get to any gigs. And so, I was never able to see the band perform at this time. Then of course, they split, and I thought, that's it, I'll never be able to hear them do these great songs live!

Imagine my excitement when I saw an advert for the Modrophenia weekend in Dublin in April 2011, which included From The Jam, Secret Affair, The Purple Hearts and THE LAMBRETTAS! I quickly rounded up a few of my like-minded friends, and tickets, accommodation and ferry were booked! What a weekend! All the bands were amazing, and to see The Lambrettas bought a tear to the eye! Outstanding! I even bumped in to Doug and Amanda backstage which was great!

At this time, I had just started arranging concerts in our small but beautiful 17th century hall here. The reason being was that Clough Williams-Ellis, the designer and creator of Portmeirion did not want it to become a museum, but it should be used as a creative influence! So, it was then that Amanda and I hatched this plan of bringing the

ABOVE LEFT AND RIGHT: *Portmeirion poster*

ABOVE: *Portmeirion wall of fame*

band to the home of 1960s TV series The Prisoner, which we did on Friday 30th September 2011! It was exceptional, and I'm proud to say we've remained friends since, and I have seen them play many times! When I was asked to help arrange the first Porthmadog Scooter Rally in 2016, there was only one band I wanted to headline, and so it happened on Saturday 28th May of that year!

I feel very honoured to have seen and met this wonderful band, and long may they continue!

There were a few gigs during 2010 where we learnt some hard, but vital lessons. In retrospect they are quite funny, but at the time, not so! I won't mention which gigs they were, but 2 particular ones are pretty memorable!

The first one was a lesson in how you must contact the sound people in advance and check on PA, etc. We arrived at this venue and the soundman was rather worse for wear (not necessarily always a problem, but in this case, he must have smoked a couple of acres of weed!) They did their sound check and, after some time, they decided it was probably best to just go with a mix that was the best we could hope for in the circumstances. When it came to stage time, they went on, the soundman was at the front, and I was at the side behind a pillar. Half way through the first song Doug was giving me a look that something was wrong, and there was pretty bad feed-back. I looked round the pillar, no soundman! So, I went to the lady on the door and asked if she knew where he was. She said; "He's gone to do a disco that he booked last week!" I was gobsmacked and panicking. There were a few friends there, Mik and Sue Boon, and Dave Walker. Dave played in bands, so I begged him to come with me to the desk, and between us we twiddled some knobs and got rid of the feedback. That was the best we could do!

Mik and Sue Boon: Sue and I first met in 1979 as young mods aged 19 and 22. We married in 1980 at the height of the mod revival. The Lambrettas were one of our favourites from that era, we bought every record and loved them on Top of the Pops and dancing to their hits. Thirty years later, and we first met the Lambrettas at a gig in Harlow with Long Tall Shorty. Soon after Harlow we saw them again at the gig with the infamous disappearing sound man at Scunthorpe! We became good friends from then on with the band and Amanda, and meet up regularly over the years at gigs. Thanks for a lifetime of great memories.

Mik and Sue Boon

Dave Walker: I remember being so excited when 'D-a-a-ance' came out, especially on Picture Disc. As a young 16-year-old Mod it felt so fresh and new and it, along with the 'Beat Boys in the Jet Age' album, seemed to be permanently on my turntable. I joined the fan club and was thrilled when I received a personal letter back from 'Jo' who ran the club. I still have the Jet shaped enamel badge and the fan club badges I bought back in the day. The years went by and I joined an online forum at one point, reminiscing about days gone by. It turned out that this was run by one Mark Ellis, former bass player, who had moved to the USA. We exchanged quite a few emails and Mark sent me some original memorabilia, stage passes and tickets along with a very rare Jet shaped metal badge. He even sent me Christmas Cards!

I was delighted when Doug and Paul put a touring band back together and felt a bit awestruck to get the chance to meet them outside prior to a gig in Scunthorpe. As it turned out I ended up on the mixing desk that night as the "sound man" had deserted

his post. Through the power of social media Amanda ('Jo') managed to track me down to say thank you, which began a great friendship with the band. I have been privileged to sing live on-stage with the band performing the Anthemic title track from that first album on several occasions, making an old man very happy and that 16-year-old Mod's dreams come true. *The Lambrettas, so sure in what they do...ABSOLUTELY*

Dave Walker performing Beat Boys with The Lambrettas

The second lesson we learned was always get a deposit. We drove almost 300 miles to do a gig and didn't get paid! We were new to this and it was booked for us, so we assumed all would be ok. Not only was a deposit not paid, we also booked the hotel, hired the van, petrol, etc. So, we paid out a fair bit to go and do a gig. When we arrived, the guys seemed pleasant enough, but had absolutely no idea what they were doing. The venue and sound people said these so-called promoters were on the dole and

The Lambrettas and Modern Works

didn't have any money. We knew it was going to be difficult and they nearly didn't go on stage, but we decided they had to as otherwise the people who had bought tickets would lose out as well. So, both The Lambrettas and the other band, Modern Works, went on and did great sets. The guys had to be chased down at the end by some of our friends who were at the gig, and they gave us a cheque which they promised wouldn't bounce!! It obviously did, as we knew it would. Modern Works, the venue and the sound people all had the same problem, so goodness knows what happened to the ticket money! Still, you live and learn.

We decided around 2011, that when possible, it would be good to take a Roadie with us to gigs. We didn't know anyone who was free and knew what to do, so the first person who came along was mine and Doug's son Ben. We always tried to get family or friends as we knew they would help us as much as possible. We had a couple of other people who came to a few gigs with us occasionally, and then Stuart Booth was our next permanent Roadie from 2014 until 2016. After this we had our mad French Roadie, Yannic Grangier until 2017, when Ben came back to do most of the rest of them. There have been funny times with everyone, but the language barrier with Yannic made for some of the most difficult, but hilarious episodes. His command of the English language wasn't as good as it could be, however it was so much better than our French was. What he didn't tell me until much later was, when I was explaining things to him, he was nodding and saying yes, but actually he never had a clue what I was talking about!

| *Ben Roadying* | *Stuart Roadying* | *Helen and Yannic* |

Ben: When Dad got back together with Paul and the others in 2009, none of us had any idea that they would still be playing 10+ years later! So, the first year or so, I went with them to some gigs where they didn't have a Roadie. Then when I went to Dublin in 2011 and met Andy, Edd and a few of the other stage and sound people, I saw how useful it is to have someone; not only to help move stuff around, but also to be at the side of the stage in case anything goes wrong. So, from mid-2011 I went along as a

Roadie whenever I could. I had to stop for a few years from 2014, but have been back since the end of 2017.

Yannic: At the beginning, I accompanied Helen which is my fiancée to the gigs. After a while I started to be the roady for The Lambrettas. So much beautiful memories and so much very stressful sometime like during this gig in Scotland. It was in Kilmarnock. The audience was absolutely crazy and quickly the dance floor was

Putting up the Lambrettas banner

like a swimming pool full of beer. I was afraid for the members of the band, the floor completely damp, and it was possible to slide and to fall down. So I decided to go outside to search something to dry the floor. But when I returned with a mop and a bucket, the door was locked and no handle outside. S...!! I knocked on the door but with the sound, no one hear me. I was in total panic! So I tried to call Amanda for a several times, but with the music and this crazy audience, Amanda hadn't hear the ring. So I decided to find another entry by the pub just near-by. When I arrived at the bar with my bucket and my mop, I said to the barmaid, "Sorry I am French and I need to clean the dancefloor". She said... What?? Sure she was thinking WTF with this French man. So finally I found a way to return to the stage. I was just between the band who was playing and this so crazy audience who was dancing with my mop and my bucket to try to dry this swimming pool. *It's not easy to be a French roady!! It was the best period of my life. Thank you so much to The Lambrettas for all the fantastic adventures across England, Wales and Scotland!*

On stage at Kilmarnock

Scottish Trip

Helen: Funnily enough I started seeing my French boyfriend, Yannic who is a big fan of Mod culture just before our first gig in Lewes, and I asked the band to sign the Lewes Live poster afterwards to send back to Yannic in Brittany because I knew he'd love it. Mods do like their memorabilia, and of course he framed it straight away! Later on, he came and Roadied for the Lambrettas for a while.

We also sell merchandise at gigs when we can. It doesn't really make a fortune, but helps towards paying for rehearsal expenses, etc. We also didn't have anyone who could do this, so Cheryl, Paul's girlfriend took it on. Sometimes, when Cheryl isn't able to do it, we have a guy called Nathan who comes with us. And Rob Wright (who we met at the first Brighton gig) also sometimes does it for us. Whenever possible, they have helpers, especially if we are at bigger venues. Often, the merch areas are shared by other bands, most particularly Sandra from The Chords UK and Tracey from Secret Affair.

Rob Wright with The Lambrettas

Merch: Amanda and Cheryl

Merch: Cheryl and Sandra Pope

Merch: Tina Coombs and Cheryl

Cheryl: I first started organising the merchandise for The Lambrettas around 2013. It came about because I was going with Paul to gigs anyway, so I seemed the obvious choice for someone to set up and sell it at gigs, and it was keeping it in the family which we like to do within the Lambrettas. Paul and I sourced a T shirt seller, sent him the logos, and it went from there. We gradually added in badges, cd's, etc. as we went along. From time to time we try a few different things. Some are popular, and some not. We actually had some woollen beanie hats for a while, and they were proving to be difficult to sell, until one summer we went to a festival that was next to a river, and as dusk came, there were swarms of midges like you wouldn't believe. Everyone was getting really badly bitten, and I sold quite a few of those woolly hats that day in the middle of summer!! I always prefer it when I have a helper, but this only happens if there is someone who is coming anyway. The same when I share the area with other bands merch sellers, it's always more fun.

Emily Flood: I've only been going to The Lambrettas gigs since 2018 when I first met them. When Ben goes to do Roadying, I go and help Cheryl do the merch. I have only done a couple of gigs, but enjoy helping out as I feel part of it, and it gives Cheryl the opportunity to get a break.

Merch: Emily Flood and Cheryl

Nathan: Working for a couple of years out on the road gigging round the UK with the Lambrettas often meant crawling back home a few days later in the early hours of dawn after a trip away with the band on tour from varying music festivals and live music venues. One of several funny outings was an incident where myself and a mellow crew member, Stu were sharing a roll up containing the international herb, out of a hotel room somewhere in the north. We were being sensible so ensured to smoke outta the window so as not to upset the hospitable landlady of the establishment. Without a second thought the end was flicked outta the rooms window only for it to fly in slow motion straight down towards the street which unfortunately overlooked the gigs entrance where the security door bouncer was stood and it bounced straight off his head! A quick duck'n'diving ensued, with muffled laughter from our room and a slowly closed window. The angry doorman came thundering through the venue looking for a culprit to take out some ugly vengeance on, thus, me n Stu decided it was time for lights out and managed to survive another entertaining evening!

My top two favourite outings were Portmeirion and the 100 Club. At Portmeirion we had a great host (Meurig) who took us on a guided tour in a golf buggy, and the great Welsh pub we stayed in under the Snowdonia mountain views, where the landlord looked after us and we had a lock in. My friend; trombone player Dan, turned into a demon pool player that night who never missed a shot. The 100 club; having never been to that venue before, and being an old school northern hippy raver, the small sticky well used basement place was the real deal. *I also met a few other bands merch sellers, who were a great crack and made my job that evening*

Merch: Nathan

very enjoyable. I can certainly say the Lambrettas were a real pleasure to have worked with and left some fond memories of eventful nights on the road.

Sandra Pope: Nothing made a Mod girl feel cooler than being on a dance floor and flicking her head from side to side, having the points of her perfectly cut geometrical bob swing across her face. One song that was perfect for that was 'D-a-a-ance' by the Lambrettas. 'Beat Boys In The Jet Age' was one of my favourite albums from the Mod Revival, full of danceable catchy pop tunes. Fast forward to 2013 and I'm standing in front of a stage watching them play their songs live! Albeit just Doug and Paul being the only original members still in the band, but giving the songs the same love and passion nearly forty years later…and I danced!! As the merch girl for the

Merch: Cheryl and Sandra Pope

Chords UK, I have got to know the Lammies very well and have spent many enjoyable gigs standing at my merch table next to Chez and Amanda singing along to the bands and watching the fans have a good time. They are the kindest, most down to earth people who took me under their wing and showed me the merch ropes and I love it when both bands are on the same bill. *I look forward to many more gigs with the Lammies in the future.*

Tracey Wilmot: The Lambrettas – Beat Boys, Power Pop and Me. As a young mod girl most of my friends were boys as the mod scene was pretty much dominated by male fans; suited and booted lads and there weren't many girls into the scene. My favourite bands were lovingly tippexed onto my parka as a tribute; among the bands that achieved this accolade were indeed The Lambrettas and my green army coat still hangs in my wardrobe as a treasured icon to my youth.

One of my earliest memories of The Lambrettas was a night I didn't even manage to get into see them, my diary records the reason was the venue was over-run with skinheads who had targeted the show in order to cause havoc. I queued for ages to get in and had an altercation with a skinhead girl who tried to start a fight with me and was

not expecting me to fight back. Seeing the dangerous situation unfolding my mod mates decided not to venture in, and I reluctantly followed them. At this point The Lambrettas were on a wave of success following the 'Beat Boys In The Jet Age' album which was a masterpiece; and still remains one of my top five favourite mod albums of all time. I recall Jez Bird as an unconventional mod, red suits, tie-less and bouncing about the stage with great energy. 'Poison Ivy' was brilliantly covered, but it was those lyrical masterpieces that Jez and Doug crafted that caught my ear, 'D-a-a-ance', 'Cortina MK11', 'Another Day Another Girl', I can still recite every single lyric to this day, and I still get a buzz out of hearing the audience sing along

Merch: Cheryl and Tracey Wilmot

to every tune on that brilliant power pop/mod album.

I was sad not to have met the front man Jez Bird due to his untimely death, but I do recall the first reunion shows with Doug Sanders on vocals while supporting Secret Affair shows. Doug literally leapt from the stage at one point and the audience loved it dancing along with him and singing the choruses. What a night that was!

Over the years the band have become great friends and with the merchandise, I have had the great pleasure to work alongside Cheryl and Amanda supporting sales of both bands and enjoying the banter with fans and sharing great memories. I'm sure that Jez would be proud of the legacy he left behind and is still dancing *"into the twilight zone"…TRACEY WILMOT*

At this stage it is probably the time to go through all the band members who have been involved from 2009 to date.

In June 2014, Chris Venzi-James decided he was not able to commit to playing with The Lambrettas any longer. Luckily, we had a natural break until September, so were able to find a new bass player, Nick Beetham and rehearse him in. We did some great gigs with Nick, but then in December, 2014, he sadly decided he also was not able to commit the time, as his job was too demanding. However, he agreed to stay until we found another new bass player. In the end Nick found Ant Wellman for us. Ant rehearsed-in pretty quickly, so Nick only had to do until mid-February 2015, and then Ant took over at the end of February that year. Ant was still with us until the last gig to date on 27th May 2019. However, he decided he no longer wanted to continue, so when/if The Lambrettas get back out there doing gigs, there will be yet another new bass player. Not sure why, we just don't seem to be able to keep bass players!

In 2015, The Lambrettas were booked to do Lewes Live Festival on 11th July. Because it was a home town gig, Doug wanted to put on a good show, so we decided to get a brass section to play with them for this gig. Back in November 2014, they had borrowed the brass guys from Secret Affair to play 'Poison Ivy' with them at a London

Gig at Under the Bridge with Secret Affair's Brass

Lewes Live Festival with Brass Section

Brass: Dan Rehahn, Helen Kane

Brass: Dan Rehahn, Mark Mansell

Brass: Helen and Mark

Brass: Mark, Helen, Dan

gig, and they all agreed what a difference it made. We contacted some people around the area, and we ended up with Dan Rehahn on trombone, Helen Kane on trumpet and Mark Mansell on saxophone. They rehearsed in a couple of songs, and all went really well at Lewes, so they decided to keep the brass section whenever they could. Dan, Helen and Mark did a couple more shows in 2015, and then from 2016 there

Brass: Dan and Richard

Brass: David, Dan, Richard

were always some brass included at the gigs. Always at least two, sometimes three. Mark left in September 2017 as he had personal commitments, and Helen moved to France with our French Roadie at the end of 2017. From 2018, sax player Richard Anstey joined Dan, and the two of them played through until the last gig and are still members. Finally, in 2019, David Medland joined playing trumpet, so they were back to having a full 3-piece section.

Helen: I was living in Lewes when I was asked about playing with the Lambrettas for their appearance at the Lewes Live Festival in 2015. I was like "wow! how cool would that be?" Doug wanted a brass section for 'Poison Ivy', 'Watch Out I'm Back' and 'All Day and All of the Night', so I got in touch with fellow busker Dan Rehahn, and we found Mark Mansell, and we all just went for it. We hadn't played together before, but there was such a fun vibe between us from the off. It was only meant to be

The Lambrinis

the one gig, but we obviously did something right because we eventually became a fixture and lo and behold '**The Lambrinis**' were created!! Although at Lewes we only did three songs, as we became more of a permanent fixture, we added other songs to our repertoire until the brass section were on stage for the whole set. Me and Dan have a bit of a cabaret spirit somewhere, (what with our busking backgrounds) so we always added a few spontaneous moves and grooves to the mix. One thing is sure, we had fun from the start and that (along with the great songs of course) is what made it work so well.

Helen and Dan moving & grooving

Helen and Dan moving & grooving

After the mistakes we made in the first couple of years, by 2011, we were more experienced with bookings. Over the years we have still had some weird one-man-

and-his-dog type gigs, everyone gets those, but also some absolutely great ones. Some of these were in unusual venues and also some great festivals.

Scott Sunyog: Top 40 Wonder Kid to True Blue Glory Boy – My Odyssey into the Mod Revival and the Music of the Lambrettas.

I grew up in a house surrounded by music! Dad's accordion, Mom's 50s 45s, jazz greats and the big bands (Buddy Rich and Maynard Ferguson). At twelve I was headlong into home taping off the Top 40 album-oriented Rock FM Radio. At boy scout summer high adventure base in 1981, a friend turned me on to the 'Who's Next' album which played continually throughout our camping trek and the rest is history! I had to have more...

Back home I made a direct beeline to the local used record store and found a used copy of the 'My Generation' LP along with the Richard Barnes book Maximum R&B. This was my window open into the world of mod and the mod revival – the clothes, fashion, clubs and of course the bands that were name checked in the book. I pillaged through the used record shops in Chicago to find releases by two bands specifically called out – Secret Affair and The Lambrettas. The records and singles were very hard to find in Chicago in the summer of 1981, but I was determined!

Four months of scavenger work finally landed me 'Behind Closed Doors' by Secret Affair, I wore out the grooves! Then a few months later, out of all the places, a discount pharmacy chain called PharMor had a heap of $1.00 cassette tapes laying in a bin. After spending a few minutes putting aside numerous copies of Rick Springfield and Soft Cell tapes, it finally hit my eye – the 'Beat Boys' release. The quality of the physical tape itself was pretty subpar even for the times but the music hit an immediate chord with me. The strength of the songs, the arrangements, the soulfulness and upbeat nature of the tracks and the variety of the grooves. That tape lasted me 20 years with lots of TLC to keep it intact.

Fast forward. My career in international banking afforded me the benefits of travel abroad. I was blessed enough to spend a lot of time in London, the Mod Mecca. Carnaby Street (Sherry's, Lambretta Shop) the 100 Club, 229, Camden, I soaked it all up! The early 2000s gave us The Lambrettas anthology on Sanctuary, my first listen to many of the singles and the second LP. This release was on standing rotation at our home, sound-tracking backyard parties, BBQs, special events and many evenings sitting by the fire. As luck would have it, a 2012 business trip coincided with the Modrophenia event at 229 The Venue – my first time seeing the Lambrettas live! I still have the sticker that Doug threw into the audience during their set along with the setlist that I grabbed from the stage! Their sound was perfect and the energy fuelled my motivation for many weeks to come.

Meeting my heroes was a dream come true and I finally had that opportunity in 2015 at the 'Beat Boys 35th Anniversary' gig at the legendary 100 Club. Great memories, discussions, camaraderie and shared musical interests forged a special friendship going

Scott Sunyog and Doug   Scott Sunyog and Phil   Scott Sunyog and Paul

forward. I did my best to plan my trips to London around Lambrettas gigs and I often succeeded in that endeavour! Great music, great people and timeless memories. Thanks, mates, for all you do and here's to many many more special times ahead! *KTF! Scott Sunyog, Darien, IL USA, August 2020*

Doug: Having got to know Scott over the past few years, I'm really flattered that he likes the band. He's an extremely talented musician – saxophone, piano, etc. To be honest I'm also somewhat surprised. Both of us have some serious jazz leanings, both fans of the Brecker Brothers, Spyro Gyra, Miles Davis and many more, including my all-time fave band Steely Dan. So, to think that someone likes who I think are some of the best musicians on the planet and also likes The Lambrettas, I'm lost for words. It is also nice to have an opinion from someone from across the pond. *Thanks Scott.*

Paul: It kind of escalated after Brighton and was completely unexpected. We had been going to do a one-off gig and there we were playing regular shows around the UK and occasionally some rather fun European shows. Also, we went and recorded some new

Marbella fun   BBC Radio Cornwall

tracks, and we did a live radio session at BBC Radio Cornwall. For me now, I'm glad that it happened again and most shows are really good fun and mentally rewarding.

Doug: When we reformed permanently in 2009, it wasn't like the manic days of before, I wouldn't change any of that, but at the time, it was hard to take it all in. It seems a little more relaxed and paced now and I know that is partly down to being older. Also, the logistics are a bit more chilled and there is no pressure put on us, including by ourselves. Some things to me remain the same. I've always only really thought about music and fun. I've never correlated it in any way with success or money, and I just consider those things a handy bi-product if they happen.

Nick Beetham: I remember my time playing with The Lambrettas very fondly. Even though I only played for 10 or a dozen shows, it was a very exciting time. I'd been an amateur musician for a while, accustomed to playing pub gigs and similar, as well as a handful of festivals and this was great opportunity to contribute to the band and gain more experience of playing new material with professional players – I'd have to raise my game! I really enjoyed meeting Amanda, Doug, Paul and Phil at the audition and, after we'd played a short set of songs that Amanda had sent me to learn, they more-or-less offered me the gig there and then. That was a big moment for me. Our first gig together was on my birthday and in Hastings – my hometown! I really enjoyed learning (original bass player) Mark Ellis's bass parts – highly figured and interesting to play and it was superb fun to play the songs with the band.

Butlins, Skegness, 2014

The schedule was quite busy – after Hastings we had a show on the outskirts of Birmingham where we were the first act to play in the newly-refurbished venue (and our

Looe Festival 2014 with Pauline Black from The Selecter

signatures were the first on the wall in the dressing room, freshly painted for the purpose). Other gigs I remember being in The Drill Hall in Lincoln (a really nice venue), The Dome in Liverpool (after a hellish road trip on the M6 to get there), a couple of weekenders at Butlins in Skegness, (brilliant fun – huge rooms full of people going nuts) and in Milton Keynes, Dartford and Crewe. All the gigs were fantastic experiences – I'd say my two favourites were at the Looe Festival in Cornwall (where the house backline was a huge Ampeg rig – my favourite!) where we played with The Selecter and Brand New Heavies amongst loads of others; and at Under The Bridge at the Chelsea football ground. That was rammed and it was great to 'borrow'

Gig at Under the Bridge

Secret Affair's horn section for 'Poison Ivy'. We did quite a few gigs with Secret Affair – by coincidence I'd known Ian Cairns (David Cairns's brother) and his wife Liz before joining The Lambrettas. *I loved my time playing with the band.*

Unfortunately, having a demanding day job and being in the band (and being committed to both) meant that each started to get in the way of the other so I had to make a difficult decision to call it a day. However, I'd known Ant Wellman for some time and suggested him as a possible replacement and was delighted that he turned out to be a perfect fit.

Nick Beetham

Gig at Under the Bridge

Mark Mansell: I spent two brilliant years touring with the Lambrettas and in that time we played at some amazing places to some lovely crowds.

A few stick in the mind; the weekend in Marbella, memorable for several reasons, primarily because it was the first time I had flown in over twenty years! It was a brilliant weekend and all the people there were so welcoming. The gig itself was amazing, there was a great crowd and at the end of it someone wheeled a Lambretta on to the stage for some photos. There was plenty of R&R and I'll admit I had a few Desperados and it was nice to chill out with the rest of the band.

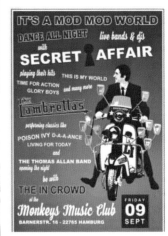

Sabinillas, Marbella

Flyer Hamburg

Sabinillas, Marbella

Another good one was Hamburg, I worked out that we did Gatwick to Gatwick in just shy of 24 hours. It was another gig alongside Secret Affair, great turnout and gig, plus we got to watch them after we had played.

The alternative music festival at Skegness Butlins was another goodie. We played to one of the biggest crowds I'd ever played to. It was a great crowd and another memorable weekend, and after a couple of large vat's I ended up in the mosh pit in front of Sham 69.

I'm proud that I was given the opportunity to do some recording with them and having it put on to vinyl. One thing I never thought I would be able to do!

All in all, it was a very memorable time and I met some lovely people, musicians and fans of the band.

Steve Goodey: 1980, I was a 15-year-old Mod living in Essex, I had the parka, the tonic suit and loafers and a love of great music. This was the year that people really got to hear of The Lambrettas. 'Beat Boys in the Jet Age' was released, an album I still consider to be one of the greatest albums of an era. Four great singles were released from that album, and there could have so easily been more. Jump forward to around 2013, I was now living in a small town on the Spanish coast when I hear the unmistakable noise of two, two stroke engines and I get to make friends with owners Alex and Aurora. Turns out Alex is a northern soul and ska DJ and he introduces me to Gary, another Lambretta owning expat and member of the Sabinillas Scooter Crew. Little did I know that this would be the day that would lead me to reacquainting myself with a scene that I left behind many years ago, and with The Lambrettas. We had organised a couple of rallies, the scooter scene is still big down here, but for 2016 the 3rd Sabinillas Rally, we wanted to bring a couple of bands to town and hold a free concert on the

The Lambrettas with Steve Goodey's friends, Sabinillas

beach. Secret Affair had played in Valencia the year before, but for us there was only one choice and on 13th April 2016 after a lot of hard work arranging flights, hotels and transport The Lambrettas took to the stage and performed in front of a packed sea front. Now here lies the caveat to this story. After a year of hard work going backwards and forwards, promoting and selling advertising to get the money together to put on the show, a week before the concert, I was sent to the Philippines for six weeks by the company I work for. I have been a fan since the 80's and was a driving force in getting this arranged and now, I was going to miss the whole show, Gutted is not the word! I have since seen the band live in London, they still put on a great show, and Beat Boys is never far from my record player. I would like to personally thank Doug for recording some intros for my on line radio show on Radio Mix based here in Spain. It was a great experience organising the gig and an amazing honour to be asked to add my memories to this book.

Ant Wellman: I joined The Lambrettas in February 2015 replacing my friend Nick Beetham who had decided to move on. I did my first gig in Portsmouth the same month, where, in my newly acquired stage clobber of sharp whistle & flute and hat, I first heard the name 'Hiesenberg' (the main protagonist from Breaking Bad!), which came from David Coombs.

Over the next 4 years we gigged all over the UK and Europe where we had some memorable gigs in Italy, Germany and Spain: sitting with the lads and a few beers in beautiful Valencia, being cooked Paella beachside in Marbella and playing at the Lambretta anniversary at the Formula 1 track in Monza. Other memorable gigs for me include The Great British Alternative Festivals at Butlins, Skegness and Minehead, they were always a blast. Another that sticks in my mind was The Brook in Southampton.

In 2017 we recorded the 'Go For It' EP which was the first release of new songs from the band for some 35 years. To have a vinyl release (a first for me) was super cool too.

I will always smile remembering the overweight and clearly in terrible health bus driver who picked us up at the airport in Germany, we wondered how he was going to drive us with his wooden leg, which as it turned out he couldn't as he hit the only post in the car park on the way out. Spending hours in a bus driving to Scotland in the blazing sunshine until we hit the border when it started thrashing it down with rain. Post-gig meals in Indian restaurants, rooming with Phil who'd always have a couple of comedy DVD's and we'd sink a bottle (or two!) of the finest Red wine (or whatever Red was going!), Paul's head glowing like a snooker ball after a potent bowl of Nachos with Jalapeno peppers, one of the reasons why, unless you were poor Cheryl who had no choice, rooming with him was to be avoided at all times!

David Medland: I was introduced to The Lambrettas by a friend and colleague of mine, Guy Denning, who has recorded the band at his studio in Kent. I had shared a dressing room with them in Bristol a couple of years previously while I was playing trumpet with the Dub Pistols, but we were all just passing through. Now having met, and played with them, every experience I have had with The Lambrettas has always made me walk away feeling the better for it. As I'm writing this, I'm listening to the voice recordings in my phone memory from the first rehearsal I made with the them on 18th Feb 2019, which has as much infectious energy as any live gig with a full audience. I have only played one gig with them (so far), Mods Mayday at Islington Assembly Hall in 2019, but I was made to feel so welcome, chatting backstage, etc. The gig itself was a real blast, in fact not just The Lambrettas on that day, but everyone within the scene, from the other bands (we were all in the same green room), to security and audience. I'm really pleased that I am playing with a band that has created such excellent music and who have welcomed me so warmly. *Thanks Lambrettas, I'm looking forward to more!*

Richard Anstey: Ironically back in April 2018 I'd been in isolation for several weeks, due to a mad bug. The phone rang and it was Doug Sanders saying that I'd been recommended to him to play sax and would I like to audition for the Lambrettas. It was a Thursday as I recall and Doug invited me to audition the following Thursday. I

Richard's pic of Dan from back of stage, Islington 2019

immediately discharged myself from hospital on the Saturday, rather than wait for the Monday when I was due to go home. At least I had 3 days to learn the tunes. In hindsight I must have been mad, but the lure of playing 'Poison Ivy' was too much of a temptation. Anyway, it all worked out and I was delighted to be asked to join the band, especially as it meant I could hook up again with incredible bass player Ant Wellman.

Our first gig was the Mods Mayday 2018,

with Secret Affair and The Chords UK, which was a brilliant introduction to the 2018 Mods scene, exciting and electrifying, especially as it was the band's 40th Anniversary coming up in 2019.

However as is the way of things fate intervened and as 2020 dawned, we were all looking forward to starting up again, but then Covid arrived on our shores and the world began to meltdown.

Although, on a positive note I have learned through playing for The Lambrettas that I should not accept drinks from sound engineers and I should never share a bedroom with Paul!

Doug: Since we reformed on a permanent basis in 2009, we've done a lot of gigs, some brilliant, some as per, and the regulation derelict pub in the middle of nowhere with no advertising and attended by 2 people and a dog. Even these we still treated the same, and in fact had some real laughs. There have also been some gigs we've done which have corresponded with the death of various music artistes. I don't care about genres or decades, that also includes my taste in music.

100 Club Audience singing "I believe in Miracles"

We should all respect those people who have entertained so many, and we try to give a little nod to those we have lost during a gig if it's appropriate. One night at the 100 club Errol Brown from Hot Chocolate had sadly died a couple of days before. Late in the set we launched into 'I Believe in Miracles'. The audience were great and all sang the line "you sexy thing". It was a great tribute.

Doug; (Purple Festival) So many good ones it's hard to pick out favourites, but the

Purple weekend Flyer

Purple Festival in Leon, Spain had a massive and very eager audience. There were lots of bands and we were on the last night, second on the bill to The Buzzcocks, who incidentally were brilliant. We were there for 2 days and even the 2 to 3-hour coach journeys through the mountains, the hotel and immense airport delay were memorable. I was very saddened to hear of the loss of Pete Shelley, but have some good memories of him, Steve Diggle (what a nice fella), and the rest of the band.

Doug; (Looe Music Festival) Probably the gig at number 1 for me was the Looe Festival in Cornwall. It was brilliant on every level. The entire town is taken over and it is amazingly picturesque. The atmosphere is as good as I've felt. I remember being recognised a few times whilst wandering about in town, which is very flattering for a z-lister like me! Everyone seems to be a passionate music lover. In 2012 we played on the Beach Stage at about 6.00pm. I thought that it might be a bad slot, but the weather was great, the beach was rammed and the audience were really responsive. I really like it when you get them to sing along, which we did quite a few times at that gig. There's nothing like everyone getting involved. I remember The Levellers (another bunch of

Looe Festival flyer

Brighton reprobates) played that night and the audience were still full tilt. We stayed in a caravan park on the hill above Looe, but we had the most amazing dressing room for

Looe Festival 2012

the evening. It was a whole cottage right in the town all to ourselves, about 3 minutes from the beach. We were also really well looked after by Nicola and Tanya. We played there again in 2014, which was also a great gig. I know it has since changed its name and organisers, but I hope we can play there again one day!

Nicola Eckersall: I worked with Looe Music Festival for 4 years and had the pleasure of looking after The

103

Lambrettas on all the times they attended. Friends made for life. It was great to meet them and see the crowds enjoy their performances. We then arranged for them to play at Carnglaze Caverns in Cornwall which is the most amazing venue. It was an absolute pleasure to have been able to meet you all and still be in contact. What a wonderful journey you have had!

Phil; (Carnglaze Caverns) That was an unusual one – playing in a cave! It was summer 2013, just a few miles from Looe where we played in 2012 and 2014. Inside was a big space and a very exciting place to play, but as we walked down the hill into the cave you could feel the temperature changing and it was so much cooler inside. At the soundcheck we started to notice all the moisture dripping through the ceilings and the walls. When it came to the gig itself the acoustics of the room made it quite challenging as it was like playing in a giant bathroom. Also, every bit of electrical gear had bits of polythene over it to

On stage at Carnglaze Cavern

stop the water creeping in, and the massive mixing desk must have had moisture inside it as throughout the gig random instruments or vocals would shoot up in volume or disappear from the mix! It was a crazy gig but really nice to play somewhere so unusual, and great to be back in Cornwall.

Carnglaze Cavern sound check

On stage at Carnglaze Cavern

Phil; (Dunoon) Dunoon was a great gig. The previous year we had done a couple of Scottish gigs, and although I enjoy them, the massive amounts of driving are tiring, but this time as it was a one-off, we were able to fly up to Glasgow. We were collected in a minibus, and the driver explained about the local history as we drove out of the city. Still on the minibus, we caught the ferry across to Dunoon, an amazing picturesque landscape. We arrived at lunchtime and played that night. The stage was right on the water's edge, a fantastic spot. It was a great weekend because we had all the following day to do some sightseeing. This is a very rare occurrence on a gig weekend, as we are

Dunoon Ferry, L-R:
Helen, Dan, Paul, Phil, Doug, Ant

Dunoon

Dunoon

usually up first thing, breakfast, then drive 300 miles home. This time our flight was not until the evening, we were to be collected by the minibus at around 5pm which gave us all day. We all split up and did our thing, mine was some walking through the hills, an absolutely beautiful place. Final memory; Ant and I bought some wine and cheese and we sat on the seafront stuffing ourselves and enjoying the view. Oh, and we didn't even mind too much that the flight from Glasgow was delayed by a few hours!

Cheryl; (Great British Alternative Festival, Butlins, Skegness) At one of the Butlins gigs in Skegness, I was selling merch at the front of the stage and The Lambrettas had just finished their set. All of a sudden Chris Waddle, yes Chris Waddle the footballer was at the merch stand! He said, "*How can I get backstage as I really want to meet The Lambrettas*". This has to be one of the only times I've been star struck as I'm into football and I had a crush on him in my teens. I said "*Give me a minute*" and I ran backstage to find Amanda; "*I need a backstage pass really quickly*" I said. I didn't want him to disappear while I had gone. She gave me one and I ran back to get him. I took him backstage to meet everyone. Me and Paul hung out and had a beer with him at the end of the night. We even got his phone number.

ABOVE RIGHT: *Cheryl and Chris Waddle*

ABOVE CENTRE: *Cheryl and Amanda*

RIGHT: *Flyer*

Cheryl; (Upton [Sunshine] Festival) This festival started early and we had arrived about midday. Bad Manners turned up so we were hanging out with them. The Lambrettas went on late afternoon. We stuck around to watch Bad Manners. After the gig we all partied into the night with the backstage staff. We ended up calling everyone Dave. The next day Myself, Paul and Mark (Paul's son) decided to go back

Cheryl, Don Powell and Paul

to the festival for the day rather than drive home first thing. We were backstage and Paul said "*OMG there is Don Powell*"! He is one of Pauls favourite drummers. We chatted to them for a while and I managed to get a cheeky photo of Dave Hill.

Paul; (Festivals) In recent years we have played at quite few festivals and events. A particular highlight for us has been the Butlins weekender events at Minehead and Skegness, which we just love. The Butlins show that really sticks in my mind is the first Great British Alternative Festival at Minehead in 2012 on their Centre Stage. We opened the

Butlins 2013

Butlins 2018

evening session at 8pm and to be honest had no idea how we would be received. We had not had even a glimpse of the crowd and were told to be in position ready to play as the curtains were opened after we were introduced. We just couldn't believe the reception we got and the room was heaving with about 2500 people. I was in my element and just played my heart out. I think it was only about an hour set but it seemed to go by so fast. It blew my mind to see people at the front singing along to every word. Whilst mentioning the singing along crowds, another thing that had me totally in awe was some of the European shows we did. They knew every word!

Paul; (Mods Maydays) Another of our absolute favourite gatherings are the Mods Mayday events. An event with great mod type bands, and of course we fit right in. These events seem to sell out most years and just get bigger each year. Up until 2017 we played the 100 Club, the 229 in 2018 and Islington Assembly Hall in 2019. Other bands on the bill are pretty much all our old mates like Secret Affair, Chris Pope's band The Chords UK, Squire, etc., so we have a blast backstage and of course on stage too. They have only been in London so far, but we all agreed it would be great to tour it around the country. In fact, we all talked about this with Adrian Gibson (AGMP), the events promotor, but unfortunately now this wretched Covid virus is with us, who knows what is gonna happen.

Mods Mayday

Mods Mayday

Ben; (European gigs) It's quite difficult to choose favourite gigs, as we always have a real laugh. I go with them on most of the European ones as mum doesn't like flying, so as well as doing the Roadying, I have to do all the logistics, admin, etc. on the ones she doesn't come on. At times it's like looking after seven school children, all with completely different behaviours, some good, some bad! Not that I'm one to talk either. I've liked going to Italy, Spain and Germany as well as the ones around the UK and Ireland. One that springs to mind was actually a private event! It was at a wedding just outside of Berlin. We arrived at Berlin airport at 9.00am, so we had the whole day before they were playing at the wedding party in the evening. We were collected at the airport and taken to the venue, which was a very large area of woodland with lakes and a couple of main buildings housing the hotel and reception area, and lots of 3-bedroom prefab chalets, which we had one of. The complex was obviously part of the former East Germany and was an amazing place. The groom, Marc, met us at the complex when we arrived and he took us out for a bite to eat. We had schnitzel, and that's the only meal I've ever known Wincer not to finish! It was massive. Marc really looked after us for the whole trip, and it was a great weekend. The next day we weren't flying back until the evening, so while the others were chilling at the complex for the day, I said I would go with Paul to visit his daughter who lived in Berlin at that time. We met her, and spent some time with her, and then after we had walked her back to the railway station to see her off, Wincer discovers that he's lost his wallet! We didn't have much time, and had to backtrack our entire route for miles, and luckily found that he'd left it at an outdoor bar, just sitting on a table. When we eventually arrived at the airport, the others were all there panicking, and we just caught the plane with minutes to spare! We had a gig later that year in Hamburg, and we put Marc and his missus on the guest list. I like that we often make friends who we see at gigs again. I also really enjoyed the one at Sabinillas, Malaga where we also stayed for a long weekend with sunbathing time

Marbella   Monza

Monza

the next day. And the Monza one! It was the Scooter Club Lombardia 70th Anniversary World Rally, and it was actually at the Autodromo Nazionale Monza, and was held in the paddock just behind the parabolic curve. Mum overcame her flying phobia for this one! There were so many scooters there on show, and we went and sat in the stands for a while as they had a ride-out for the scooters on the circuit, and there were also some cars doing practice runs. The guy who was organising it all gave us an anniversary badge.

Flyer

Lechlade Festival

In 2017, we went to play a Festival at Lechlade-on-Thames in Gloucestershire. We made a few more friends there; Jennie, who organises the festival, Donald Cartwright, who made us the most brilliant meal in his restaurant, and completely went above and beyond to look after us, even though he was desperate to get to the festival! Also, Eric Hobson, who was a mod back in the day, who took some great photos.

Lechlade Festival

Eric Hobson: Never referred to myself as a mod, others did that, as they could identify us with the way we dressed, the scooters and the music. More importantly, it was a way of life that identified a person as being in the group. Music was important and often new music such as Ska (I was also a drummer in a band at that time). 60 years on, what remains of that lifestyle?... I still have a liking for expensive clothes, particularly Paul Smith, I am sure he was a mod. No chrome scooter but replaced with a classic Porsche 911. Still have that love of music from that period, but also a liking of new music particularly World Music; Ska was world music so not so surprising. We were a band of the 60's but still living the life.

Dan Rehahn: My favourite Lambrettas memory is of visiting Porthmadog, in Wales in 2016. The only reason I was available for this particular gig was that I had turned down an offer to play for the 'Christian' festival near Chanctonbury Ring, in Sussex.

I played there one year, having been seen doing trombone karaoke in Gardener Street, Brighton.

I was booked to do a solo performance outside between stages, which I did, over two days. They asked me back the next week (for the following year), and I said "No". My reasoning was, however much money they offered me, I didn't wish to be a part of their Christian Zionist experience.

The Lambrettas have always treated me with the utmost respect.

I bought the LP 'Ambience' on the internet, and the dealer in the Netherlands (whose name now escapes me) wouldn't give my money back, despite my futile attempts to provide forensic evidence that my copy was warped and would not play.

Since then, having been ensconced in my record collection (recently fortified by finds in the local skip), some of the songs have become playable, by virtue of flattening the vinyl over time – 'Decent Town' as recommended by Ben, is a particular gem, but also 'Concrete and Steel'.

Not to mention 'Total Strangers'...

I also admire the nude tango dancers on the cover...they remind me of a Sardinian lady who I still adore.

Anyway, we had a great time in Wales, thanks to everybody concerned. Xxx

Porthmadog

Helen: It was always an adventure to go off on a Lambrettas road trip, but the best thing about them was the variety. The gigs themselves were fantastic obviously, but it was also a bonus to discover the venues backstage too. I loved White-haven Mining Museum in Cumbria and the Winter Gardens at Morecambe, just as much as I loved the Grand Prix racing track at Monza in Italy and our exotic beach-side gig at Malaga in Spain. Ben came to roadie at Malaga, I'm told the trouser incident at the airport was after-sun being applied? No matter where we were, the crowd were always up for it, and we were lucky to play some fantastic venues in so many different places.

Ben Marbella Airport

Like Dan, a great memory for me was our trip to Porthmadog. Yannic and I nearly ran out of petrol in the Welsh mountains before we even arrived! We had a great gig the night after and it was topped off by our personal trip round Portmeirion with its legendary location manager and friend of the band, Meurig Jones, who is just wonder-fulness personified. It really is one of the most incredible places on earth — a unique universe full of follies, tall stories, and breath-taking views.

100 Club

Just about to go on stage at Butlins

The Lambrinnis with Yannic

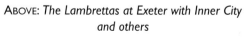

ABOVE: *The Lambrettas at Exeter with Inner City and others*

Right: *The Lambrinnis with Yannic*

113

I have to give my full respect to Amanda for managing to routinely round-up a brass section with a terrible penchant for wandering away just when we were needed to be in the same place at the same time (i.e. soundcheck). Maybe we were secretly tagged, but she definitely had a knack for appearing just as we were about to disappear on food/beer/adventures and say *"you're not going anywhere are you?"*

I loved our Mods Maydays at the 100 Club. Just the best venue ever.

Some of my favourite gigs have been:

(Snowdonia Scooter Rally) We went back to North Wales to play at the Snowdonia Scooter Rally event on 28th May 2016. Once again Meurig was our contact and organised things for us, along with Kevin Tiernan and Lewgi Lewis. As before, some of us travelled up the day before. This time we stayed in Porthmadog at The Queens Hotel, where Derek Williams looked after us all for a couple of days. In fact, Meurig, Kevin, Lewgi and Derek couldn't have done more for us. This time, Dan, Helen, Ant, Yannic and Nathan came for the first time. Again, on the morning of the gig Meurig took us on a buggy tour of Portmeirion and the others fell for the charms of The Village too.

Snowdonia Scooter Rally 2016

(City Hall, Salisbury) In November 2014, The Lambrettas played at the City Hall, Salisbury, along with Secret Affair. I've picked this gig for two reasons; firstly, it was when I decided to write this book, even though I didn't start it until 2020. The second reason was that Andrew Gilbert's son did the lighting for this gig, and Dave took photos, as he

City Hall, Salisbury

quite often did. The lighting and the photographer produced some great photos that night.

(Skamouth) Finally; Skamouth. In November 2012, I was contacted by this guy called Tom Fahy, who was putting on a new event the following year with a girl called Christine Coffey, now Staple, married to Neville! They had teamed up with Vauxhall Holiday Park in Great Yarmouth and they were thinking of calling the event Skamouth. The Lambrettas played on 19th October 2013 at the very first Skamouth! That first event was a success, and Tom & Christine have organised two every year since. We were booked again for 21st April 2017, and 23rd November 2018. I love going to the Skamouth events, they are so laid back and inclusive between the bands and the audience. I normally have quite big stress on gig nights until after stage time, but Tom, Christine and the crew make it an experience that I enjoy even beforehand. All the audiences are brilliant as well (they are there for the whole weekend) and you can just stop and chat with anyone, whether you know them or not! The Lambrettas usually go to the café in the morning to do a breakfast chat with anyone who is there. At the last one they did, they were interviewed

First Skamouth Flyer

Amanda and Cheryl
at Skamouth

2017 Skamouth Flyer

LEFT: *2018 Skamouth Flyer*

RIGHT: *Skamouth Flyer Chris Watts
with Doug*

BELOW LEFT: *On stage at Skamouth*

BELOW RIGHT: *The Lambrettas and
Gary Shail having breakfast at
Skamouth*

116

by DJ Chris Watts, who had interviewed Doug for his Meridian FM Radio show previously. This was an event that our friend Gary Shail was at as well. Chris's flyer for the next Skamouth included a pic of him interviewing Doug and it just makes me laugh, which is why I have included it.

Where legends and friends WILL meet again!

RIGHT: *Skamouth Mixed Artist photo*

Christine 'SUGARY' Staple, Performer, Song-Writer & Event Director; & Wife & Manager of Neville Staple, From The Specials & Fun Boy Three: Working with the Lambrettas over the last 8 years has been a real pleasure. They are a regular favourite at the Skamouth Weekender festival that I run, with my colleague Tom. We have a mixed crowd of mods, rudies, scooterists, soundboys and skins, as well as people who just love the revivalists of the 70's and especially the 80's. I have often performed alongside the Lambrettas too, at gigs and festivals across the UK, with my husband Neville Staple (From The Specials). Both bands share the same fanbase and also the sharp fashion of dapper suits or cool sportswear. Being a late 60's baby, I grew up with the most amazing sounds as a teenager, from Trojan Reggae, to Punk, Ska, Mod Revival and New Wave, and over my later years, I have become a lot more aware of just how brilliant all this was. We were so lucky. The Lambrettas for me, are even better now than they were during the Top of the Pops years, like many bands from that era. When you're still going live and direct to fans, all these years on, your music will have grown and matured into something so very special too. Artists like The Lambrettas have become even

Skamouth: Neville Staple, Doug, Christine Staple

bigger experts, of their very own expertise. This, alongside the nostalgia of yesterday and the retro and new fan adoration, makes for top-rate, musical performances. These guys are brilliant and *I will always be ready to 'Listen, Listen, Listen,' and 'D-a-a-ance'!!*

Tom Fahy: For me, 'Poison Ivy' was my introduction to the Lambrettas via Top of the Pops back in the day. It was also played extensively at just about every pool match I attended, through the tannoys of the day, reinforcing it as a seminal sound of our scene. The music of the Lambrettas has been with me ever since those days and continues to be an inspiration to do the things I do, when putting on the Skamouth weekender events with my colleague Christine.

Skamouth: Tom Fahy and Amanda

Towards the end of 2011, we were contacted by a guy called Kevin Crace. At the time he was working for a company who had bought the rights to some ITV archives, which included the Lambrettas concert filmed in Nottingham for the Rockstage programme in 1980. The company were going to release it on DVD and Kevin was the contact to agree how this would work with us. Although the DVD was sadly never released, we became friends with Kevin. We met him in person for the first time at the Great British Alternative Festival, Butlins, Minehead on 28th April 2012. He came backstage to discuss the DVD with Doug and Paul.

Butlins Minehead 2012

Kevin Crace: The first time I had reason to speak to the Lambrettas was back in the sunny days of 2011. I had been engaged by a record label to seek out a number of historic acts to see if I could arrange for them to cooperate with us on a series of live albums. Normally I dread working with bands who have a history, but the Lambrettas were the absolute exception to this rule. From the moment that I spoke to Doug and his wife Amanda, who manages the band, the three of us just gelled. I was stunningly refreshed by how easy they were to work with, how professional they were and how they understood both the music industry and their place in its grand history.

2012 saw me take a road trip from London to Somerset, to see the band perform live for the first time. It was one of those Butlins Music Festivals. An amazing line up of bands as I recall, The Damned, Anti Nowhere League, Blockheads etc. But to me The Lambrettas blew them all away, no question. They were tight, professional, note perfect and they knew how to take the audience with them. Meeting them backstage for the first time was nothing but a pleasure. They treated me with total respect and the hand of friendship. From these initial and tentative enquiries, we were soon able to come up with a plan with my client, to work on the glorious ITV recordings of the band captured back in 1980.

Kevin Crace

Dave Coombs: The late '70s were an exciting time in music. As young teenagers we had grown up with home grown Glam Rock in the early to mid '70s as well large American/British 'stadium' bands. All these bands were out of reach to go and watch live, being too expensive and only playing large venues well out of the reach from Aldershot (my hometown) 1977 changed that! All of a sudden there were hundreds of new bands with a new sound and musicians my age, Punk had arrived. I loved the sound of these new bands and we now had our own 'local' bands (The Stranglers, The Jam, The Members and Sham 69 all within 15 miles of us). Although a great sound I found the whole punk scene a bit frustrating and it seemed to be full of pretentious middle-class kids trying to out-do each other with more and more outrageous behaviour and a lot of designer punk outfits, as well as the fear of extreme violence if you went to a gig. 1979 saw a complete change in direction, mainly down to the film Quadrophenia. The Jam had been quick to nail their colours to the mast of this new tribe with a nod to the 60's with sharp suits and a clean-cut image. The music was still fast and exiting but you could dance to it. More new bands started to appear on the scene and the so called 'Mod Revival' had arrived. Being 19 and able to drive meant I could now travel out of my town up to London to see these new bands. The Greyhound in Fulham being a favourite place to meet and see a band. This was the only time I saw The Lambrettas back in the day. I think it was before the band released 'Poison Ivy' so they weren't yet on their winning streak and before the release of their debut album, 'Beat Boys in the Jet Age'. Exciting times.

Fast forward to about 10 years ago at the Alternative Music Festival at Minehead in Somerset. I was now a photographer and had been invited to photograph Bruce Foxtons band From the Jam. This allowed me access to photograph all the bands, where again I was reacquainted with The Lambrettas. Although Jez Bird was no longer with us, Doug Sanders was on vocals and drummer Paul Wincer were still holding their places as the original members of the band. It was great to hear all the songs again which brought back a lot of youthful memories of a great scene.

I sent all the pictures I had taken to Amanda, the band's manager (and Doug's wife), and a new friendship was formed. This has resulted in me photographing the band all over the country many times since. I occasionally help out on the merch

Dave Coombs, Paul, Cheryl, Tina Coombs

as well as a bit of gear humping. *Forty years on they are still going, and still sounding great, as well as being able to pull a regular crowd of us oldies that still remember the phenomenon known as the Mod Revival.*

Stuart 'Spud' Goodwin: I first saw The Lambrettas on Top Of The Pops with their version of 'Poison Ivy' and was blown away by it, not only was it a great, catchy song, but by their clothes too. It was immediately apparent that these guys were one of the leading packs of the new Mods that were coming along and I wanted to be a big part of it. Records were bought by the handful, clothes were begged and borrowed and with a scooter to follow I was there.

Sadly, I never managed to get to a gig back then and with the untimely death of Jez it seemed highly unlikely I ever would. However, fast forward to 2011 and there was suddenly a buzz in my home town of Lincoln that they were going to play after a scooter event in the city.

They played a blinder that night, all the old favourite songs were blasted out by Doug on vocals, Paul on drums and a couple of new guys Phil Edwards on guitar and Chris

Venzi-James on bass. A great night was had by a packed crowd, but due to circumstances I didn't manage to meet the band, apart from a quick handshake straight after. I did however manage to get a good record of the night as I took quite a few photos of the night. My first experience of photographing bands and it's all down to The Lambrettas that I got the buzz for it. Here is one of those first photos.

Lincoln 2011

The next time I saw them was again in my home town, supporting Secret Affair on their Glory Boys 35th Anniversary tour in 2014. Due to the fact I knew the promotor and my photography hobby now being almost an obsession, I was asked to be the official photographer of the night. At last I was able to meet the band and became friends very quickly, and what a terrific bunch they turned out to be.

I saw them twice in 2015, first in Cambridge where they were supported by The Circles and the second in Grimsby where they supported Secret Affair once again. We were in for a surprise that night when they announced they had added a brass section for some of the songs, and that produced a new, terrific sound for the band. A new face on bass also gave the band some Ant Appeal with Ant Wellman joining for a more consistent line up. With my photography habit expanding I was again able to shoot quite a few (dozen) photos at both venues, including some backstage with the band having some funny moments with the fans.

More great nights have followed at the Mods MayDay events of 2018 and 2019 where it was great to meet up again with old friends, listen to the songs that were so familiar from our youth that you can sing along with, and also a few new numbers that were released on the record 'Go 4 It'. These gigs were full to bursting with friends, some that go back up to 40 years and some new ones too, all having a fantastic time. Many more photos from these gigs show just what a great time we had.

Stuart "Spud" Goodwin

The last time I saw any of the band was at Brighton 2019 for Gary Shail's Quad 40 event which saw Paul guesting on drums and Doug doing a short but excellent vocal spot with The High-S which was one of the highlights of the show. As usual I was there with my camera in hand to shoot a few of their guest spot. I have something in the region of 1,200 photos of the band that I can look back on and enjoy, hopefully there maybe one or two that will make their way into the book for all to enjoy.

In October 2013 Kevin rang us and said: "Does Doug want to go in the Identity Parade on Never Mind the Buzzcocks tomorrow?" He knew he would get the p… taken out of him, but said yes anyway. Jez had done it previously on series 17 in 2005. Unfortunately, we were unable to find any film of Jez online, but probably thanks to Huey Morgan having his mug smashing meltdown, the one that Doug did was repeated several times and is easy to find online. We had loads of phone calls that day from the wardrobe people at Talkback to get his sizes for the clothes. On Tuesday 22nd October Doug and I drove up to the studio in Camden. We were given a dressing room and Doug was not allowed out of it in case Phill Jupitus, Noel Fielding or anyone else on the panel saw him. He was allowed to be smuggled out once to have a cigarette, and had to get past Roger Daltrey and his entourage, who had come to promote a box set of 'Tommy' that was about to be released. The runner who was looking after Doug was really panicking in case he got lost in the melee, but he got back without a problem. The show is actually recorded for much longer than the 30 minutes it airs for, so we were watching it on the screen in the dressing room, and Doug had a panic at one point! I had to block the door so he didn't run away. Then when he got his call, I went up to the green room to watch it from there. The comedian Paul Foot picked Doug out of the identity parade! The episode aired on 4th November, it was Season 27, Episode 7. Kavana was on the other identity parade.

Never Mind the Buzzcocks

In June 2013 we were contacted by a guy called Darren Hall from Portsmouth. He was acting on behalf of two ladies Steph and Lisa who were putting on an event at the Portsmouth Pyramids venue. It was for **Tonic Music for Mental Health**, a charity based in Portsmouth. Their mission statement is; "*We raise mental health awareness, challenge stigma and promote mental wellbeing through music and the arts*". We had not heard of them until this point, but The Lambrettas played at the event on 12th October 2013, and we have kept in touch ever since and like to support Steph and her brilliant charity whenever we can.

Tonic Festival, Portsmouth Pyramids

Steph Langan: I booked The Lambrettas for a fund-raiser event in 2013 for my charity, Tonic Music for Mental Health. The event was held at Portsmouth Pyramids and had sold out. The Lambrettas were on a line up with Bonehead (Oasis), From The Jam, Dub Pistols and Terry Hall (The Specials). I vividly remember meeting Doug, Paul, their lovely wives Amanda and Chez, and the rest of the guys at the back of The Pyramids. Lisa (Tonic co-founder) and I were waiting to greet the band and show them to their dressing room. This was a new thing for us – putting on gigs and meeting bands, as mental health practitioners we were more accustomed to working with people in distress. We were genuinely nervous that day and I remember the band being so incredibly lovely to us. They were down to earth, warm, friendly and genuinely pleased to be part of our fundraiser. I will always remember Amanda saying to us "*I've never seen promoters looking so relaxed*". I think that has stuck with me six years later because we didn't feel relaxed nor see ourselves as promoters but that comment gave us confidence. The Lambrettas played a blinding set to an eager crowd that night who delighted in their mod revival songs. It felt incredible watching the band. They had time for everyone, signing photos, chatting to fans and taking time to find out about our charity Tonic. We swapped numbers that night and have stayed in touch ever since. The Lambrettas continue to support us at Tonic. They've played subsequent fund-

Tonic Music for Mental Health Shop, Portsmouth

raisers, visited our shop and give us encouragement. I'll forever be chuffed that The Lambrettas played our first sold out gig and even more proud to call them friends. *Steph, Founder Tonic Music for Mental Health.*

In 2014 The Lambrettas were inducted into the Brighton Music Walk of Fame. It was really nice to be recognised and they felt proud to be included. Doug, Paul, Fiona and I went to a launch party on 17th June 2014 at the Brighton Wheel which is now no longer there. At that time they had pavement-plaques in the form of vinyl albums along the south side of the promenade of Madeira Drive.

The Brighton Wheel

*Brighton Music Walk of Fame
2014*

Doug, Paul and Fiona Bird

The Lambrettas have shared a stage with a lot of bands over the last ten years, most of whom have been around as long as them, The Beat, The Selector, Bad Manners, The Buzzcocks, Toyah and Neville Staple (From the Specials) to name just a few. They also play regularly with Secret Affair and The Chords UK and we have become good gig friends with all of the guys, their crew and merch people, as well as Squire and The Deep Six, along with other mod bands.

Helen: I guess there aren't many female trumpet players in Mod bands, or even girls in Mod bands per se, so I was happy and proud to add something different to the line-up. I love the Mod style and it gave me a good excuse to hunt down a nifty vintage frock or three. It's such a classic look, but add a trumpet and it's another layer of coolness. Our brass section was made up of three distinct individuals and personalities, but as a whole I think we added some playfulness as well as some

Messing about at Whitehaven Mining Museum

'oomph' to the proceedings. You can't be really cool if you take yourself too seriously.

Steve Wilkinson (from Inner City): And they say you should never meet your musical idols! There are certain albums and songs that capture your youth. Luckily for me 'Beat Boys In The Jet Age' is one of them. Pure pop, anthems and well written and performed tunes. The songs were passed on to me at a teenage party. The album I couldn't sneak under my parka that night. So, the following weekend I tracked down a copy in my local record shop as quick as I could. The cover shot is one of my favourites of the time. I sometimes wonder if the photo with the monitor screens on the beach inspired some-one in the Oasis camp years later? Those songs on that album could have spawned some great singles: 'Leap before you look', with Pauls drum-breaks, 'Living for Today' with its sing along anthems and words, 'Face to Face', a song our band Inner City have covered over the years, and 'Runaround' which Sting could have written at the time. Their follow up 'Ambience' is underrated in my eyes and ears. Go on give it another listen and see what I mean. Years later I had good post correspondence from Jez and

he signed my Beat Boys album sleeve. Since 2009 we have met up with the re-formed Lambrettas many times as a band. One time a few years ago Doug came to meet us and have a drink in our local pub in Weston-Super-Mare. We are pleased to call him a friend and he's always got time for his fans and share a story. And they say you should never meet your musical idols!! *Cheers Beat Boys.*

Doug with Inner City in Weston-super-Mare

Chris Pope: Back in the day, a long, long time ago in the year of our lord 1979 to be precise, there came along a Mod revival/renewal or whatever name tag you choose to hang on it.

126

I guess the big hitters from the scene were a couple of bands from Essex notably, Secret Affair and The Purple Hearts, and one from South East London, The Chords, and a bunch of guys from the South Coast called The Lambrettas.

As a member of The Chords, I got to know and play alongside the Essex boys a fair bit, but with The Lambrettas, not sure how, but our paths never did cross in those heady days and by 1981, The Chords were gone and so was I from the scene.

It wasn't until I put The Chords UK together some 30 Plus years later that our paths finally crossed.

From sold out Mods Mayday shows at the 100 Club, up to the Islington Assembly Halls, in 35+ degree sweltering packed gigs in Cardiff, thru open air festival madness, to bizarre 'function' room insanity shows in the middle-of-nowhere, it has always been a huge pleasure and incredibly enjoyable experience playing alongside Doug, Paul and the guys.

Unlike many a band/artist/group, with Doug there's no axe to grind, no huge ego, just an amazing, straight up friendly geezer. That also goes for all the band members, wives and girlfriends included.

Playing together in the 2010's made me trace my steps back to 1980 once again and to really listen to their original stuff. The album, 'Beat Boys in the Jet Age', including the fantastic 'Page 3', alongside their big hits, 'Poison Ivy' and 'D-a-a-ance' is a testament to their talent. Also, I have to mention the brilliant track 'London Calling' (no NOT that Clash song!). They really were a 'Power Pop' with more than a dash of R&B band of their time.

They also haven't rested on their laurels and have continued to make new music with their EP 'Go 4 It' of which the title track is a cracker and, if they don't mind me saying, is in the mold of Graham Parker and an absolute fab, good ole 'British Rock 'n' Soul' tune. Nice one!

I always look forward to seeing the guys when we're on the same bill and I hope that we can finally do that 20 date UK tour together we keep promising ourselves!

PS. I'm still secretly dead 'jel' they got to work with Sir Elton and had Mr PWL produce their first single! Best, Chris Pope

Chris Pope on stage with Chords UK

Dave Cairns: Back in the day when the Mod Revival became a news story in the music press and the tabloids, Secret Affair had been doing their own thing at the Bridge House in Canning Town and The Marquee Club on a residency basis. Before then we only found out about other bands through word of mouth and fanzines. We heard about The Chords from South London, Purple Hearts from Essex and a Brighton band called The Lambrettas. Despite being relatively near to each other our paths never seemed to cross at the time, and that included our TOTPs appearances when we'd appear on different episodes.

Although never meeting back then I loved their version of 'Poison Ivy' and their album 'Beat Boys in the Jet Age' which in my view remains an underrated classic album that still sounds fresh and new to this day. A collection of brilliant lyrics and catchy tunes and it is still great to see the audiences' responses when they play 'Page 3'.

Dave Cairns on stage with Secret Affair

Since we all called it day back in the 80s it has been great to reform and be on the same bill over the last ten years with The Lambrettas and other bands from that time. We've all become firm friends, not just with the band members but also with the ladies behind the scenes, Amanda and Cheryl. We often end the evenings in the hotel bars after a great performance, and just pick up from the last time, a bit like a family. Such evenings together have taken us from the bizarre and dangerous in Liverpool, to festivals around the country and some great moments in London. I hope if we ever get over this terrible virus that we'll be sharing a stage again soon. ***Dave Cairns August 2020.***

Mackenzie (from The Novatones): As a teenager, my dad had introduced me to the 'mod' culture. Beginning with Paul Weller and The Who, I grasped onto this movement and delved as deep as I could, discovering the early music that inspired the Mod culture itself. Rhythm and Blues, Soul, Be-Bop, Mod Jazz and so much more entered my world as fast as I could find it. Fred Perry, Ben Sherman and Levi's filled my wardrobe, suits and ties meant more than just school uniforms and Quadrophenia was the go-to film whenever the TV was on. Just like the movement itself evolved with every resurface, so did my discoveries. Mod revival was like a lifeline for me after realizing I was born nearly 40 years after it had originally fizzled out. With that came the discovery of new bands. Purple Hearts, Secret Affair and of course, The Lambrettas. Though the genres of music that I infatuated myself with changed from Hip-hop, Soul, Folk, Indie, Punk and more, these bands always remained staple listening for me.

'Beat Boys In The Jet Age' was one the first albums I bought myself, I was so excited when I found it on the rack of a local music shop (one that, unfortunately is no longer standing). I don't think I had quite realized then that my discoveries weren't exactly niche, and that I probably shouldn't have been as surprised as I was to find it there. That album got played almost daily at one point. At the time I was at college, and during a particularly boring lesson I decided to look for more information on other releases or shows that The Lambrettas were putting on. They had no shows organized near me at the time, so I had an idea. As a student with no job and so no money to travel for shows, why not bring them here? My band at the time were modelling themselves on the Mod

Revival bands of the 80's, so I thought that a shared bill would be perfect. Finding an email, I got into contact with the guys, which culminated in a show at The Joiners in Southampton. This was the first time I met The Lambrettas. We met in the upstairs dressing room, I **was** 17 and just beginning to see what the live music scene was about, and Doug, Paul and the entire team made me feel like an equal. The confidence that I have taken with me through my performance career is in no small part down to that meeting and the fantastic people that The Lambrettas are.

Years later, my old band had reached an end and I had joined another band, The Novatones. I have so much to say about this band that I couldn't ever fit it into one paragraph, but with The Novatones I have played to empty rooms and packed festival tents, we have hit the highest highs and the lowest lows but we did it together. Anthony, our lead singer, had a slightly similar upbringing to myself. He was introduced to the Mod culture at a young age, but he carved out a different musical background, his tastes range from classic Fleetwood Mac to The Prodigy's deep cuts and obscure D&B mixes. Between the two of us, songwriting becomes such an eclectic mix of original ideas and abstract inspiration. Eventually, our path crossed with The Lambrettas, and to my absolute shock, they had remembered our initial meeting. After a few shows, we became good friends. In fact, one of the fondest memories I have of any performance is supporting them at London's legendary 100 Club. The dressing room walls and ceiling are completely full of band names, dates and slogans all written in magic marker (bonus points if you find "The Novatones" written on that night). In this dressing room, packed in like sardines, we all sat and talked about music, football and films. Like you would your old friends over a beer, which is exactly how it felt. We joined the band onstage for 'Poison Ivy', a first for the rest of the band and something that became a small tradition for me, (this is also where we found out that none of us could really D-a-a-ance…).

This show truly set in motion the wheels of our friendship with the band, to the point where Doug, a musical hero of mine, had actually called me up to discuss music and provide us some advice to navigate the music industry, through hilarious experiences,

The Novatones on the Hard Rock stage at the Isle of Wight Festival

emotional stories and advisory tales we spoke about almost everything…until my phone battery died halfway through. Had I been able to tell my fourteen-year-old self that one day I would accidentally hang up on Doug Sanders, I don't think he'd ever forgive me!

The Lambrettas are described as a 'cult band', one that has an 'underground' following. But to The Novatones and I'm sure many, many others, they are more important than I think they'll ever know. To us they are inspiration, they are mentors and above all, they are our friends. Without Doug, Paul, Ant, Phil, Amanda, Chez and everyone else we have met through The Lambrettas, The Novatones may not have been able to achieve some of the fantastic things we have. The Novatones, with all we have, hold an incredible amount of love for our friends, The Lambrettas.

Huge thanks to Amanda, for putting this together and for asking us to contribute. We are truly honored to be a part of this. *Peace and love, Mackenzie, The Novatones.*

There are always new young bands out there, some come and go and some stay around for longer, and they're all really good. However, everyone has one they like to follow whatever they are up to, and mine are The Novatones. They have been together for quite a few years, are full of energy and enthusiasm and have big highs and big lows, but still stick together through both, which is what I think a band is all about, like a family. They write their own songs, get right into performing and love their fans. Their

enthusiasm reminds me a bit of The Lambrettas in 1979 and I love that. I wish they could have had the same experiences and journey that Doug, Paul and crew did, but these days the music business is so different. Very few companies take a chance on new bands these days, which is a shame. I bet Sally Atkins would have been interested in them if they were around in 1979! Look them up and have a listen. Anyone who hasn't seen The Novatones should go and watch a live show!

The Novatones

In 2015, after some years of the original songs not being available, 'Beat Boys in the Jet Age', a 2 x CD compilation was released on the Salvo Label.

We continued to regularly meet up with Kevin over the years and he advised us on

Mods Mayday at The 100 Club 2016

some other matters regarding the re-release of all the old recordings with Fiona, Doug, Paul and Mark. In 2016 we were told again that the DVD spoken about in 2012 was going to be released, but they needed more material, so we arranged for a live sound recording of a gig at the 100 Club in London which happened on 6th May 2016. This was sent to the company so it could be released as a double package, with the 1980 DVD, although the company has still not released it to date.

Mods Mayday at The 100 Club 2016

> **Kevin Crace**: The DVD project that I started with The Lambrettas took on more monumental proportions in 2016 that involved recording the band as they are now. This was at the 100 Club, so we could compliment these earlier recordings with the band as they currently are, line-up changes and all. And whilst this project remains as yet unreleased, it built a relationship between myself, Amanda and the band. I meet regularly with Doug and Amanda over the years. Based just outside Lewes, in East Sussex, I call by on them whenever I'm in the vicinity. Another of my music friends, Herbie Flowers, the man who put the bass line behind Lou Reed's 'Walk On The Wild Side', lived very close by, so I would often meet one followed by the other. From numerous meetings, and our mutual friendship and respect for each other, we decided that I should put the band back in the studio and look at recording a selection of new songs. The material that the band was currently writing was, in my opinion, tighter and had moved on. Accordingly, 2016 saw myself putting the band into the studio to record a selection of new songs, with the capable hands of Guy Denning at the mixing desk. The resulting songs were released as the 'Go 4 It' EP, five new tracks spread across vinyl, CD and digital formats. I hope and believe that the wonderful journey I have undertaken over the last few years, with this truly great band, continues. I find them as relevant today as they were back in the day. I find them one of the easiest acts I have ever had the privilege to work with, and most of all I hope they receive the recognition that they genuinely deserve. *Viva The Lambrettas.*

Kevin financed The Lambrettas to go into a studio to record a few tracks to release as an EP. They went to a place called Granary Studios in Lamberhurst, Kent. The owner and engineer is Guy Denning.

> **Doug**: I really like Guy. I think we have a lot in common. He's very easy to work with and he makes some great contributions but never interferes. Often producers/engineers

Recording at Granary Studios, Lamberhurst, Kent

seem to lean one way or the other. I think he must be a good character judge, as he reads people quite well and knows when to suggest things and when it's best not to, not to mention he knows his technical stuff and music.

Guy Denning: Working with The Lambrettas on the 'Go 4 It' EP was an absolute joy. From the moment Ant introduced me to them all, we were having a laugh. I felt very

<small>LEFT:</small> *Guy Denning Outside Granary Studios*   <small>ABOVE CENTRE AND RIGHT:</small> *Lamberhurst with Guy*

quickly amongst friends and the recording process was made easy by the fact that they're all bloody good. Spending quite a few weeks with people, you need to get on with them to end up with a good product. I also went with them to the 100 Club to help with the live recording they did, and mixed it for them after. Doug and Amanda sometimes pop by the studio to catch up and see who we have in. Overall getting to know all the Lambrettas and Amanda was a great pleasure and I very much look forward to working with them again.

CD cover

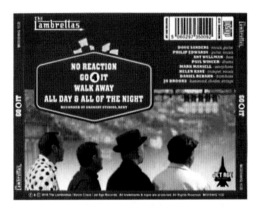

The Lambrettas Go 4 It publicity photo

Vinyl cover

The EP was called 'Go 4 It', and ended up being released as a 4 track CD and a 5 track 10" vinyl on 10th February 2017. During 2017 the CD and Vinyl were only available as a physical product, but it is now available on download as well.

133

In 2018, the Brighton Music Walk of Fame's David Courtney joined forces with the owners of the iconic Brighton Palace Pier to establish a permanent free to view cultural attraction paying tribute to the many musicians, artists, composers and DJs closely associated with the city from the sixties to the present day. The plaques were now going to be much updated, interactive and displayed on the ornate lamp posts on the boardwalk of the Palace Pier. The Lambrettas plaque was to be one of 30 displayed on the pier that year, 2018. David Courtney adds more artists plaques every year. On the 27th June there was a launch party. This time it was in Horatios Bar at the end of the pier. The main band playing was The Brighton Beach Boys, but The Lambrettas were asked to do 3 songs. Mike Read was hosting the event. It all went well and was a beautifully sunny day. This time there were 6 in the band and we took Ben to Roadie for them. Doug and Paul were also pleased to catch up with Mike Read, who they hadn't seen for 30 odd years.

ABOVE AND BELOW:
Brighton Music Walk of Fame 2018 launch party

Brighton Music Walk of Fame 2018:
Doug, Mike Read, Paul

In Mid-2019 Doug was a bit unwell, so The Lambrettas decided to take a break from live gigs for a while. The message that was put on their website said "We're hoping to be back in 2020 with a healthy band and some new songs".

Ian Taylor: 1980. Starting point. Two best mates, aged 10 are inspired by the elder cousin of one of them to consider which side they were on, the Mods or the Rockers. One of those boys (that would be me) was already leaning towards 60s beat groups and the sharper looking post Punk bands. Enough said. Life being fickle, my mate's cousin had moved onto the next thing within months but *"Would I like to buy some of her record*

collection?" Oh, what's that picture disc single with a union jack on one side and Brighton Pier on the other? Boom! Blast Off. I was too young to go to gigs but I was sold on the music and the image. 'D-a-a-ance' became my anthem, speaking to me of the near future that I hoped would be cooler than cool and full of sharp, soulful sounds and girls. A 'Beat Boy in the Jet Age' was the thing to be.

1994/95. Fast forward. Newly single, made redundant and determined to go to university as a slightly mature student. Excited by the emergence of Britpop and the subsequent revival of interest in my old Mod favourites, I am strangely drawn to the University of Sussex in Brighton. But before that I need to earn some cash. Go into my temporary workplace buzzing because The Lambrettas have just appeared on The Big Breakfast that morning. Start chatting to a colleague called Lisa about it and she says, "*Oh yeah, I liked Mod.*" The following weeks are a blur…buying the Lambrettas CD re-releases, getting engaged to Lisa and her moving down to Brighton with me. A few months later and I hear that Jez Bird is playing a solo set in the Font and Firkin in the Lanes. I dress for the occasion and take my CD cover for him to sign. Jez is very friendly and spying the Mod gear in the audience he acknowledges me and comes over for a chat afterwards. "*Can you sign this to me and my wife?*" Can he? Not only that, but he also writes a note to Lisa… "*Please make sure that you come along next time too, love Jez*"!

Speed onwards. Saturday 20th October 2012 at the King's Hall Stoke, an event promoted by the Stoke-on-Trent Scooter Club. Reunited versions of Secret Affair and The Lambrettas are playing and is this the best news ever? It's coming not long after the once unbelievable news that Lisa is pregnant. We were told it would never happen… but we didn't expect to see The Lambos live together either! The gig is buzzing, full of Mods, old and young, and with an atmosphere to die for. Too young in 1980 but making up for it now! Jez has sadly passed but Doug steps slickly up to the plate as lead singer and Paul still bangs those drums just right! Pow! They say that you shouldn't meet your heroes, right? But Amanda Sanders invites us backstage to do just that and what legendary gentlemen Doug and Paul really are! Beers offered (cuppa for Lisa), photos and, "*oh, would you sign this CD cover, please?*" Now it's got three of the original names on it…must start stalking Mark Ellis one day! The atmosphere is relaxed, the chatter is

ABOVE RIGHT: *Paul, Lisa, Ian, Doug*
RIGHT: *Darwen Live*

chilled and, I must confess, we were late getting back out to watch the Affair, we were enjoying ourselves so much!

Final flash forward. Zoom! Lancashire, 27th May 2019 for Darwen Live! and my six-year-old daughter Tilly is there with me to close the circle. 'Poison Ivy' is already one of her favourite songs ever. It's a decent crowd for the open-air event and I am in seventh heaven. The music was always vibrant and exciting, the movement was always cool but this band are part of my life, part of my family's lives. *This is more than just music. This is meaningful. This is magic.*

Although not up to doing any gigs later in 2019, Doug, along with Paul, was asked by Gary Shail to attend his Quad 40 party on Brighton Palace Pier on 25th August. It was the 40th anniversary of both Quadrophenia and The Lambrettas, and 10 years almost to the day that they had met up with Gary when they did their first reunion gig in Brighton in August 2009.

Gary wrote… *"Very pleased to announce that my old mates Doug Sanders & Paul Wincer will be joining me for my Quad 40 Party on the pier in August. The two original members of the iconic band The Lambrettas, Doug Sanders & Paul Wincer will be doing a Q&A and after a few light ales I'm sure it will be hard for them not to take to the stage to perform a couple of "crowd pleasers". This year marks the 40th anniversary of The Lambrettas, so a double celebration on that day!"*

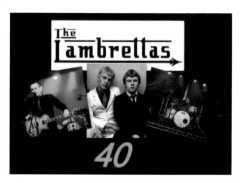

Quad 40 Advert

Gary's party was also in Horatios Bar at the end of the pier, where we had been the year before for the launch of the Walk of Fame. He had quite a few bands playing, and as well as Mike Read, there were some of the actors from Quadro-phenia who sat with Mike and Carol Harrison and did a Q&A. One of the bands, The High-s were expecting Paul and Doug to come and play a few songs with them. Paul got up to do the drums, but

ABOVE LEFT: *Quad 40: Cheryl, Amanda, Emily*

ABOVE RIGHT: *Quad 40: Gary Shail, Emily*

136

Doug wasn't feeling up to it, so Justin from the High-s was singing. However, in the end Doug couldn't stay sitting so he went up to sing the end of 'D-a-a-ance'.

Gary Shail: I first met The Lambrettas at a drinks party (I think) sometime in 1980 at the offices of Rocket Records. I'd been signed to this label, owned by Elton John, by an executive called Eric Hall, purely because I'd recently starred in a little British movie called Quadrophenia.

Now, I'm sure that you all know that this little British movie, based on a 1973 album by The Who, was about 'Mods,' so it would be reasonable to assume that my first single on The Rocket label would have been 'Mod Influenced.' Well, to tell you the truth, I didn't even know what that particular musical term meant at that point. But these lads from Brighton dressed in Fred Perry's supping lager whilst surrounded by very camp effeminate record executives, certainly knew what it meant. Within weeks of our first meeting, their single 'Poison Ivy' had reached no 7 in the national charts, whilst mine was banned by the BBC and cast into the 'not even a 1 hit wonder' bin, as were my early ambitions of becoming a bonafide pop star!

Fast forward 29 years!

In 2009 I was now a bloody 'Mod God' whether I liked it or not! Quadrophenia had secured its place in history as the life changing cult youth phenomenon that it is often described as. I was now constantly being asked to attend mod events all over the country where, more often than not, I would know absolutely no one! Then one day I was asked if I'd host an event in Brighton, where one of the very first 'Mod Revivalist' bands had re-formed to play their first live gig in almost 30 years. When I found out that it was The Lambrettas, I jumped at the chance.

The venue in Brighton was packed with mods, most who only knew this band by reputation. Also, only two of the original members had survived, Doug Sanders, and drummer Paul Wincer, so when I went backstage to see them before the show, they looked nervous as fuck! I went out, picked up the mic, slagged off the doormen, and said, "Ladies & Gentlemen the one and only Lambrettas" and they have toured ever since!

After that gig we started seeing each other all over the place at events and also socially. In 2019, I was preparing for the biggest event I'd ever done. It was the 40th anniversary year of Quadrophenia's release. As soon as I was booking the bands for the event, I was on the phone to Amanda (Doug's wife and manager of the band) telling them that they would be headlining. I couldn't believe it when she told me that they couldn't do the gig due to one of the band attending a family wedding. I was gutted. But then I had an Idea! What if Doug and Paul could play 'Poison Ivy' and 'D-a-a-ance' with one of the other bands booked to play? I called Justin Fox from the band The High-s and asked if they'd mind learning those two songs!

On the day of the event, Doug wasn't very well. I had seated Paul and his lovely wife Chez, along with Doug and Amanda close to the stage though. I explained to the band that Doug was un-well, but Paul would still be playing. Justin said that he knew the songs. Of course, there was no way on earth that Doug could sit there, so once they started playing 'D-a-a-ance', he was out of his seat quicker than a

Paul and Doug on stage with The High–S

fucking greyhound and up on the stage! The crowd went ballistic. It will remain as one of the highlight memories of that day for me, as I know it does for many others who were there on that glorious day. *So, a friendship spanning 40 years that continues to grow.*

Another person we have been friends with right since the beginning is Eddie Piller, DJ and managing director of Acid Jazz Records. He has been an influential key figure on the scene for quite some time. He used to come and see The Lambrettas play in the 79 & 80s era, and his story is back in part one. Now, we often cross paths as he has compered some of the shows we have done over the past ten years. The last time we did a show with him was Mods Mayday at Islington in 2019.

Mods Mayday 2019 with Eddie Piller

At the beginning of 2020, we were thinking it was probably time to start thinking about gigs, but the coronavirus put paid to that for the time being. Obviously, all live music stopped from mid-March, and on Thursday 2ⁿᵈ July, we joined other UK musicians in signing letters to the government, demanding action to prevent "catastrophic damage" to the Live Music Industry, using the hashtag #LetTheMusicPlay, and sharing pictures of recent gigs on our social media.

#Let The Music Play

At the time of writing this, the Culture Secretary Oliver Dowden has confirmed that indoor performances with socially distanced audiences will be allowed again from today, August 15 2020. I'm not sure how this will work in most of the venues that The Lambrettas play at, but I hope that all our friends in the industry, behind the scenes as well as at the front, will be able to get back to doing what they do as soon as they can. I know it will take some time and the 'new normal' (hateful phrase!) will be very alien for a while, but let's hope that one day soon we will all be out the other side and we'll be meeting up at gigs again.

I asked a few of 'the usual suspects' if they would like to say something. They are spread throughout this book, and here are some more. Doug often says to audiences *"If it wasn't for you lot coming along, we wouldn't be here, so thank you."*

Mick Yates: I followed The Lambrettas right from when they formed in Brighton in 1979 with Jez and Mark. Although they played their final concert on 14th April 1982, in 2009 Doug Sanders and Paul Wincer reformed to do a one-off gig, and are still going. My favourite songs are 'Beat Boys in the Jet Age' and 'London Calling'. They are by far the best band of the revival, and there were quite a few, but this band stuck out for me. Off stage they are some of the nicest people I have ever met, Doug and his wife Amanda and family, and Paul and his partner. I went to a gig in Leeds in 2010 and they invited me back stage and we have been friends ever since. I have seen the band many times over the years at various locations and hope to see them many more times. This band have always been hard working and deserve more credit than they get, although they do have a plaque on the Brighton Walk of Fame at Brighton Pier. *Thanks guys, for the music and the memories, long may they continue.*

Mick Yates with Doug

Mick Yates

Sara Farah: The first single I bought by the Lambrettas was 'Another Day, Another Girl'. I bought it from a second hand record shop in 1984 at the age of 13. I am still enjoying their music and going to their gigs 36 years later. They are the most friendly band on the scene. There was one gig I went to in Rotherham and only a dozen people turned up. The band wasn't disheartened and Doug kept shouting *"We are the mod, we are the mod"* instead of mods! It was funny, and was a brilliant gig.

Sara Farah with Doug

Alan C May: It was mid-79 and I was just getting into the mod Revival scene, living in the small market town of St Ives, Cambridgeshire, 40 or so miles from London where the movement had taken off big time with every teenager you saw in the street wearing Harrington's, Fred Perry T shirts, desert boots and parkas around every corner. There were lots of bands that appeared very quickly bursting onto the scene like Secret Affair, The Chords, Purple Hearts, Squire, Merton Parkas and of course The Lambrettas. All those bands, along with The Jam were the most standout mod revival acts at the time. They all had a number of singles which were released relatively quickly and they all produced fantastic albums Secret Affair had 'Glory Boys', Purple Hearts had 'Beat That', The Chords had 'So Far Away', Merton Parkas had 'A Face in the Crowd', but for me one of the most standout albums at the time I had, would have to have been 'Beat Boys in the Jet Age' by The Lambrettas, the most successful Mod revival chart act. I remember buying 'Beat Boys in the Jet Age' in 1980 and thinking to myself just how good this album was and how impressed I was by the various sounds that were recorded on to this wonderful piece of vinyl - my favourite tracks at the time were 'Leap before you Look', 'Beat Boys in the Jet Age', 'Runaround' and 'Page 3', later to be called 'Another Day Another Girl', due to The Sun newspaper not realising a marketing opportunity when it was staring them in the face. I thought the band were very smart, always dressed in suits with Jez Bird being a great singer on the main vocal and guitar, Doug Sanders on guitar and vocals always looked pretty cool, the ever-sharp Mark Ellis played bass and Paul Wincer on the drums. From the album the band put out a couple of tracks that would get chart success ahead of the other revival acts, 'Another Day Another Girl', the delightful swinging track 'D-a-a-ance' and 'Poison Ivy', The Coasters cover which got into the Top 10. Each track sounded different, which is a testament to the band's ability to pen great lyrics and write superb music, though personally I wasn't a big fan of 'Poison Ivy' at the time, I actually believe the Lambrettas did a much better version than the original and made the song their own, but to this day I'm always amazed that the single did so well not only for The Lambrettas but also The Coasters as I believe it was a song about catching a sexually transmitted disease! I love the honesty of the band and the way all their songs sounded different with their catchy guitar riffs, fantastic bass lines, and vocals that you could sing along to. The band certainly caught the moment in time with the high energy teenage anthems that reflected the mod Revival. To sum up the album 'Beat Boys in the Jet Age', I would say that it is one of the albums that has certainly stood the test of time and I still play it today 40 years later. The second album which was also on Elton John's Rocket Records label was 'Ambience' and was a change in direction when I wanted more from the Beat Boys style, that said there were a couple of standout tracks again like 'Decent Town' for me, 'Ambience' and 'Good Times'. In 1985 a third album called 'Kickstart' was released. This was a compilation of all what I believed were the Bands best work. One of my favourite tracks was 'Go Steady', that to me was probably the Bands best ever single and of course the first one that they released. Though the mod revival was initially from 79 to 82 and was relatively short-lived, there was something about the scene and the way the music got under your skin that made you feel you were part of something. You could sing along to these tracks as if they were written about you, and as a young teenager made you feel very special, being able to dress up and look smart. Of course, with Secret Affair, The Lambrettas certainly knew how to dress really sharp in mohair suits. The first band I ever saw in the mod revival were the Teenbeats. They came from the south coast the same as The Lambrettas. I think maybe The Teenbeats got me wanting to listen to bands like The Lambrettas as the south coast certainly had a unique sound and I am really glad that I did. I think the saddest moment for the band and for us, the fans, was the loss of Jez Bird who died of cancer in 2008 at the young age of 50. That was devastating for people like me who wanted the band to reform in its original format. However, we were delighted that Doug and Paul went on to reunite the band and to play as The Lambrettas, with Doug taking over on the vocals. I think Jez would have given them his blessing too! I've seen the band with this line up, with Phil playing guitar, a number of times. They never cease to amaze me just how good they are as a live act; they always play with

Alan May then

Alan May now

passion and play it just how I remember it as a young mod. The Lambrettas are one of the Bands that will stay with me forever, I am now in my 50s and I'm still listening to the album as if I was a spotty teenager who is going to rule the world. Moving to the modern day I'm thinking about the band in its current form and as a fan I am really pleased and excited that the band have released new material with the EP 'Go 4 it' which featured three new songs and are all very good in their own right. *I hope The Lambrettas continue for as long as possible because deep down we are all Beat Boys in the Jet Age.*

Gary Davies: Listening to 'Go Steady' for the first time changed things for ever, it was music that I could relate to. I went to an early gig at Cardiff Top Rank in 1980. 'Beat Boys in the Jet Age' to me is as relevant now as it was in the eighties. Since then decades have passed, but the music is still with us. In the past eight years Alison and I have travelled all over UK to many places to see the band. We even went out to Hamburg and Valencia to see them. There's a story from the Valencia trip, but that's for another day, lol! It's great to see the band playing their new stuff as well. Please keep going, great memories from all the trips and gigs. *It's keeping us young!!*

Gary Davies singing along with Doug   *Alison James and Gary Davies*

Dan Turner: Watching Quadrophenia in the summer of 82 at the age of 10 changed my life for ever. I had a direction! Within two weeks I had a parka and dessert boots. Sitting on the bus two years later I spotted a lad in his parka and jam shoes. Skip a week later and I'm round his house talking all things mod. Chris Kavenah was 14 and had moved with his family from Ireland. As we were talking, he mentioned The Chords, Secret Affair and then The Lambrettas. I'd never heard of any of them, but what a great name for a mod band I thought. I instantly wanted to hear these albums, so without further ado he got the 'Beat Boys' album out and we played it all night, to his brother's annoyance! Wow, this record is amazing. Not one track made me want to skip to the next track. Chris made me a tape copy and I constantly played that album all that summer. Eventually got I my own vinyl copy. Like all my mod revival bands I played them so much as I felt I'd just missed out and I'd never get to see them play live.

Skip to 2009. I got a call from my long-time mate Shaun Walker who was the drummer in my band J60. *"Ello Dan. You'll never guess what, The Lambrettas are doing a one-off gig in Brighton next month, and I've secured an interview with Paul and Doug for my Web page. Do you fancy coming?""Errrrmmmmm Yep!"* We met Amanda Sanders at the venue door and she took us back stage for the interview, and to meet Doug and Paul. Absolutely lovely people who answered all of Shaun's questions with no hesitation. I was amazed with their honesty and very grateful for their time. So, with the interview over and my vinyl and magazines all signed, it was time for the lads to take to the stage.

Dan Turner back then

Jay P. Fuller: I first saw The Lambrettas in 1992 at the George Robey Finsbury Park, and then again in 1993 at the same venue. The line-up consisted of original members Jez Bird and Doug Sanders, I can't remember who the other two were but it definitely wasn't Mark Ellis or Paul Wincer. Anyway, it was part of a series of British ska gigs that were performed at the Robey, I don't remember too much about them but seeing The Lambrettas for the first time in 1992 was just excellent and they did a blinding gig again in early 1993.

It would be 23 years before I got to see them again when I turned up at a Mods Mayday at the 100 Club in 2016 to see Squire, Chords UK and The Lambrettas. They had a great line up and that was a great night out.

I did also get to see Jez Bird doing a solo gig in 2006 at a pub in Worthing, I'm not sure of the name of the venue but it was the last time I saw him before he sadly passed away soon after.

I have been to every Mods Mayday event since 2016 and London gigs where The Lambrettas have performed. Doug has spotted me in the audience a couple of times at the 229 Venue in 2018 and the Islington Assembly Hall in 2019 and has given me a mention. I have always been impressed by how well the band performs live.

Jay P. Fuller with Doug

Tony Boden: Chucking ideas around in 2012 with how to take Stoke on Trent Scooter Club further, we decided to step back in time to our youth and organise a concert with two of the biggest mod names you could get, Secret Affair and The Lambrettas. We managed to catch both bands at different venues up and down the country and both were excellent. The Kings Hall in Stoke was chosen for a venue and on 20th October 2012, with nearly all tickets sold, a fantastic night was had by all. A great night for the city and a great night for us as a club. Just an aside, The Lambrettas had played at The

Kings Hall back on 17th December 1979, 33 years previously. Both bands were professional and extremely friendly and we wish we had more time on the night to go have a drink after, but with packing away all the gear it wasn't to be. We have caught up since and love having a chat and a drink.

LEFT: *Doug with Tony Boden and friends*
ABOVE: *Doug in the audience at Stoke City Hall*

Spencer Mumford: Kicking my heels in school, trying to find my niche, my gang and my people in the late 70's just wasn't happening. I didn't want to be a Punk or a Biker like everyone else seemed to be. But then the Mod revival happened. My personal favourites, The Lambrettas gave me my music, my energy, lyrics that meant something to me and my identity. Then a summer holiday trip to Great Yarmouth fun fair was my opportunity to convert a Kiss Me Quick hat into a trilby. On returning home, girls were asking me if I was one of those Mods. "*Yes!*" I said and I was cool at last. But I was also desperate to learn guitar and so Doug Sanders became one of my guitar heroes. He had the energy, confidence and the look. Next thing I knew, there were Mods and scooters everywhere and I was part of something that felt awesome. A proud moment came during the summer of 1980 when after endless plays of 'Poison Ivy', my purple-faced army cadets Staff Sergeant, ripped the jukebox off the wall. The jukebox was dead but Mod never would be.

Years later, to my delight, The Lambrettas came to play an intimate venue close to me. I had to go and it was so worth it. Here I was, literally in touching distance of these guys and they didn't disappoint. Doug even signed my guitar for me! But the real magic for me was when my own band got to support them at Cardiff's Coal Exchange! Some say 'Never meet your heroes' but I have several times now and I can tell you that they're all so genuine, friendly and unbelievably humble.

I could talk to Doug and Paul for hours as they've told me stuff that I've never seen in print. Fascinating stuff. Never a footnote, the tireless work that Amanda and Chez do is priceless and they are absolute diamonds and great fun to be around. In fact, I'd have any of The Lambrettas family as drinking buddies.

Spencer Mumford with Doug

Barry Pulfer: Being a Mod in the late 70's and a Revivalist, one of the bands me and my friends listened to was the Lambrettas. 'Beat Boys in the Jet Age' was such a great album of this Mod era. I remember watching them on Top of the Pops, with their brightly coloured suits. We looked up to these guys, our Mod heroes. Never would I ever have thought that I'd be good friends with them 30+ years later. Back in 2012, I co-founded a Mod Facebook page, The Mod Collective. We post Mod music sessions every night and currently have 80,000 followers. I still finish my Friday night session every week, with my fave Revival tune 'D-a-a-ance'.

Through the page, I made contact with the band and often chatted with Doug and Amanda. I was invited to see them play at the 100 club London in 2013. What a great night! Doug dedicated the song 'D-a-a-ance' to me, 'Baz and the Mod Collective'. I even got to go back stage to meet the boys and get some photos and autographs. How cool was that, and what an honour. Not long after this great gig, I received a message from Paul, saying he was going to be in my area, Romford, would it be ok to drop by? I was in shock. I told my Missus,

Barry Pulfer backstage at the 100 Club 2013 with The Lambrettas

and she said "*That ain't gonna happen*", as if to say, why would he give you the time of day. I told her we are friends. "*Yeah right*". Anyway, later that evening, there was a knock at the door, and sure enough, there stood the Legendary Lambrettas drummer, Mr Paul Wincer and the lovely Chez. My head almost come off. It was very surreal, one of my heroes, that I used to watch on tv, is in my house! We chatted for a few hours, had tea/coffee and biscuits. I'd had a Lambretta round for tea! I had a massive smile on my face for the rest of the week.

Barry Pulfer

The photo overleaf is the last publicity photo we have. As soon as we can get back together, there will be new ones to include David and the new bass player. So as of the summer 2020, Doug, Paul, Phil, Dan, Richard and David are the current members of The Lambrettas. As things stand at the moment, will they be back out there playing in 2021? No-one can predict the future, but watch this space! I thought I would leave the final words in this book to them.

Latest Publicity Photo

David: I'm very much looking forward to getting out and jammin' again. I think the world could definitely use some more live music right now! Or at any time for the record.

Richard: After lockdown I can't wait to play with the guys again. Hopefully we will be as tight as the waistband on my suit.

Dan: It's very nice in St. Tropez but I can't wait to be schlepping up the motorway to Widnes, Rotherham or Penicuik. I miss my friends. And the gin!

Phil: Being in a band is a bit like being in a special club – it sometimes feels like 'you versus the world'. But being in the Lambrettas is very different as the music belongs to, and means so much to, the fans. Look forward to hitting the road again and seeing friends old and new!

Paul: The big difference to me with the new Lambrettas to the old, is quite simple and hopefully something youngsters in groups should really try to adopt. Our big secret is that we all get on! Previously, in the 80's we were under so much pressure that we often argued over silly petty things, but now you know we just have fun and love what we do. Doug and myself have never been so close, and with the other guys (and occasionally gals), in the band it's generally a very happy camp. We all love the attention we get from our fans and will gladly chat and sign stuff (except cheques or dodgy record deals!) We prefer to do it after shows though. I personally get a bit twitchy and pace about in my own little world starting usually about 30

Bristol Ska & Mod Festival, 2016

minutes before show time, plus I need to warm up on the practice pad. Doug's the same as me and has his routine, but we need to do what we need to do in order to get into the place we need to be in mentally to perform. On the opposite end of the scale, Phil seems to be fearless and laughs and jokes backstage, has a raid of the food, tunes up and then just hits the stage in absolutely brilliant form. To sum it all up for me though, I wouldn't change a thing with all I've done in The Lambrettas. It's certainly been quite a ride and hopefully there are more rides to come! *Paul Wincer, Summer 2020.*

Doug: Whilst I wouldn't change anything about The Lambrettas, it turned out very different to the musical ride I'd always thought about. Music being such a difficult thing to get into, I thought *"best get on the bus when it stops and hopefully steer it in the direction I want as much as is possible, bearing in mind there are 4 members, record company, etc., all of whom have opinions".* When I watch a band/artist I like to hear the songs I know and love, and don't have a problem with nostalgia in that sense. Equally I'm just as enthusiastic to hear new material and even the odd cover, if it is a song you really like; an homage with a different take on it. The Lambrettas have always adopted that, with members old and new, in agreement. The productivity of new songs does fluctuate, but I think it is a must to keep doing them or relevance disappears.

   When we started, we said we'd keep the band going as long as was possible. As this book suggests, there are 3 parts. The beginnings of it all, the last 11 years, and various bits in the middle. As far as this band goes, I have been a contant since Day One. I think previous members, gone for various reasons, but not forgotten, would still stand firm with the 'keep going' sentiment. 2020 has been on standby somewhat, but we have new material and are waiting in the wings.

4 door, 2 speed wipers

Finally, to everyone who has supported us, I'm truly thankful. IF THERE WAS NO YOU! THERE WOULD BE NO US! Till we meet again. *Doug Sanders, August 2020.*

Appendix 1: Gig List 1979-1982

	DATE	VENUE/LOCATION	APPEARING (Headliner first)
1	9 June 1979	Hastings Pier	Purple Hearts, Fixations, Teenbeats, Scooters, Lambrettas
2	18 June 1979	The Buccaneer, Brighton	Purple Hearts, Lambrettas
3	19 June 1979	The Richmond, Brighton	Chords, Speedball, Lambrettas
4	30 June 1979	Lewes Paddock	Lambrettas, Chaos
5	9 July 1979	The Alhambra, Brighton	Lambrettas, Chaos
6	14 July 1979	The Wellington, Waterloo	Lambrettas, Scooters
7	17 July 1979	The Music Machine, Camden	Purple Hearts, Back To Zero, Speedball, Lambrettas
8	18 July 1979	The Dublin Castle, Camden	Teenbeats, Lambrettas
9	7 August 1979	The Richmond, Brighton	Piranhas, Lambrettas
10	13 August 1979	The Global Village, Charing Cross	Mods, Lambrettas, Spyders
11	19 August 1979	The Buccaneer, Brighton	Merton Parkas, Lambrettas
12	6 September 1979	The Greyhound, Fulham	Lambrettas, Touch
13	16 September 1979	The Buccaneer, Brighton	Lambrettas, Chaos
14	17 September 1979	The Alhambra, Brighton	Lambrettas, Tonix
15	22 September 1979	The Marquee, Soho	Lambrettas, Hidden Charms
16	24 September 1979	The Bridgehouse, Canning Town	Speedball, Lambrettas
17	6 October 1979	University of Nottingham	Photos, Lambrettas, Thunderbirds
18	10 October 1979	Tracy's, Redditch	Lambrettas
19	13 October 1979	Brighton Art College	Madness, Lambrettas
20	17 October 1979	The Basement, Brighton	Lambrettas, Cheeks
21	18 October 1979	The Alhambra, Brighton	Lambrettas, Chaos
22	20 October 1979	University of Leicester	Black Slate, Lambrettas
23	24 October 1979	Hope & Anchor, Islington	Lambrettas
24	26 October 1979	The Sandpiper, Nottingham	Lambrettas
25	19 November 1979	The Alhambra, Brighton	Lambrettas
26	20 November 1979	The Nashville, Kensington	Act, Lambrettas, Malcolm Practice
27	26 November 1979	Moonlight Club, Hampstead	Back To Zero, Lambrettas, Name
28	10 December 1979	Broncs Cafe Portsmouth	Malcolm Practice, Lambrettas
29	15 December 1979	The Sandpiper, Nottingham	Lambrettas
30	16 December 1979	The Coachouse, Huddersfield	Lambrettas
31	17 December 1979	Kings Hall, Stoke	Lambrettas

32	20 December 1979	Lewes Priory School	Lambrettas
33	24 December 1979	The Alhambra, Brighton	Lambrettas, Decent Assault
34	28 December 1979	The Music Machine, Camden	Lambrettas, Malcolm Practice, Video Stars
35	9 January 1980	Hope & Anchor, Islington	Lambrettas
36	11 January 1980	Crystal Palace, Norwood	Lambrettas
37	16 January 1980	77 Club, Nuneaton	Lambrettas
38	19 January 1980	Landport Centre, Lewes	Lambrettas, Cheeks
39	22 January 1980	The Alhambra, Brighton	Lambrettas
40	24 January 1980	The Troubadour, Port Talbot	Lambrettas
41	2 February 1980	The Norbreck Castle, Blackpool	Lambrettas
42	7 February 1980	The Trafalgar, Shepherds Bush	Lambrettas, Midnight & the Lemon Boys
43	14 February 1980	The Moonlight Club, Hampstead	Lambrettas, Midnight & the Lemon Boys
44	15 February 1980	Crystal Palace, Norwood	Lambrettas
45	7 March 1980	The Golden Eagle, Birmingham	Lambrettas, News
46	8 March 1980	Brunel Rooms, Swindon	Lambrettas
47	15 March 1980	Hastings Pier	Lambrettas, Headline, Blueprint
48	18 March 1980	101 Club, Clapham	Lambrettas, Malcolm Practice
49	20 March 1980	76 Club, Burton-on-Trent	Lambrettas
50	21 March 1980	The Cedar Club, Birmingham	Lambrettas, News
51	22 March 1980	West Runton Pavilion	Lambrettas, Malcolm Practice
52	23 March 1980	The Coachouse, Huddersfield	Lambrettas
53	24 March 1980	Rotters, Doncaster	Lambrettas, Nerve
54	28 March 1980	Bloomsbury YMCA	Lambrettas, Small Hours, Agents
55	15 May 1980	Clifton Hall, Rotherham	Lambrettas, Circles
56	16 May 1980	Fusion Nightspot, Sunderland	Lambrettas
57	17 May 1980	Barnsley Civic Hall	Lambrettas
58	18 May 1980	Lafayettes, Wolverhampton	Lambrettas
59	22 May 1980	Top of the World, Stafford	Lambrettas, Nerve
60	23 May 1980	Melksham Assembly Rooms	Lambrettas, Scoop
61	24 May 1980	Town Gate Theatre, Basildon	Lambrettas, Nerve
62	26 May 1980	Northallerton Community Centre	Lambrettas, Nerve
63	29 May 1980	The Limit, Sheffield	Lambrettas, Nerve
64	30 May 1980	The Penthouse, Scarborough	Lambrettas
65	31 May 1980	Tunbridge Wells Assembly Hall	Lambrettas
66	7 June 1980	Electric Ballroom, Camden Town	Lambrettas, VIPs, Dolly Mixtures, Gods Toys
67	24 June 1980	The Marquee, Soho	Lambrettas, Vogue

68	1 July 1980	The Marquee, Soho	Lambrettas, Sta-Prest
69	15 July 1980	Locarno, Portsmouth	Lambrettas, Scoop
70	16 July 1980	Torquay Town Hall	Lambrettas, Rhythm on 2
71	17 July	Stateside, Bournemouth	Lambrettas, Scoop
72	18 July 1980	Cardiff Top Rank	Lambrettas
73	19 July 1980	Bath Pavilion	Lambrettas, Scoop
74	21 July 1980	Cromwell's, Norwich	Lambrettas
75	23 July 1980	Theatre Royal, Nottingham	Lambrettas, Billy Karloff & the Extremes
76	24 July 1980	Sands Show Bar, Skegness	Lambrettas
77	26 July 1980	St. George's Hall, Bradford	Lambrettas, Beats Working
78	2 August 1980	Palace Lido, Douglas, Isle of Man	Lambrettas
79	9 August 1980	Music Machine, Camden	Lambrettas, Daddy Yum Yum
80	10 August 1980	Brighton Top Rank	Lambrettas, Dolly Mixtures
81	15 August 1980	Bilzen Festival, Belgium	Stranglers, Urban Heroes, Katchies, Dexy's Midnight Runners, Girlschool, Lambrettas, Shirts, Kids
82	2 October 1980	Leeds Polytechnic	Lambrettas
83	3 October 1980	The Mayfair, Newcastle	Lambrettas, More
84	9 October 1980	Palalido, Milan, Italy	Madness, Lambrettas
85	10 October 1980	Palasport, Turin, Italy	Madness, Lambrettas
86	12 October 1980	Palasport, Padua, Italy	Madness, Lambrettas
87	13 October 1980	Palasport, Bologna, Italy	Madness, Lambrettas
88	14 October 1980	Teatro Tendastrice, Rome, Italy	Madness, Lambrettas
89	19 October 1980	Brielboort, Dienze, Belgium	Madness, Lambrettas
90	20 October 1980	La Rotonde, Le Mans, France	Madness, Lambrettas
91	21 October 1980	Halle de Prestige, Orleans, France	Madness, Lambrettas
92	22 October 1980	Studio 44, Rouen, France	Madness, Lambrettas
93	24 October 1980	Maison des Sports, Reims, France	Madness, Lambrettas
94	25 October 1980	Hippodrome, Paris, France	Madness, Lambrettas
95	26 October 1980	Tivoli Parc, Strasbourg, France	Madness, Lambrettas
96	27 October 1980	Volksbindungsheim, Frankfurt, Germany	Madness, Lambrettas
97	28 October 1980	Kursaal-Bad Cannstaat, Stuttgart, Germany	Madness, Lambrettas
98	29 October 1980	Kurhaus-Friedenstal, Hanover, Germany	Madness, Lambrettas
99	30 October 1980	Sartorysaal, Cologne, Germany	Madness, Lambrettas
100	3 November 1980	Gota Lejon, Stockholm, Sweden	Madness, Lambrettas

101	4 November 1980	Chateauneuf, Oslo, Norway	Madness, Lambrettas
102	28 November 1980	The Porterhouse, Retford	Lambrettas
103	1 December 1980	Romeo & Juliet's, Doncaster	Lambrettas
104	7 January 1981	Ben Hall, Rugby	Lambrettas
105	8 January 1981	The Marquee, Soho	Lambrettas, Escalators
106	9 January 1981	Goldsmith College, Lewisham	Lambrettas, Escalators
107	17 January 1981	Winter Gardens, Margate	Lambrettas, Naughty Words
108	9 May 1981	Millfield College, Street	Lambrettas
109	28 May 1981	Central Hotel, Gillingham	Lambrettas
110	20 July 1981	The White Hart, Southall	Lambrettas
111	1 August 1981	The Rainbow, Finsbury Park	Lambrettas, Hidden Charms, Long Tall Shorty, (...and others...)
112	29 October 1981	Club Carolina, Madrid, Spain	Lambrettas
113	30 October 1981	Club Carolina, Madrid, Spain	Lambrettas
114	31 October 1981	Club Carolina, Madrid, Spain	Lambrettas
115	5 December 1981	Digby Stuart College, Wimbledon	Lambrettas, Sahara Beat
116	11 December 1981	Leeds University, Leeds	Lambrettas
117	13 December 1981	Melkweg, Amsterdam, Holland	Lambrettas, Eyeless in Gaza
118	15 January 1982	Paradiso, Amsterdam, Holland	Lambrettas
119	16 January 1982	Gigant, Apeldoorn, Holland	Lambrettas
120	17 January 1982	Doornroosje, Nijmegen, Holland	Lambrettas
121	22 January 1982	The Marquee, Soho	Lambrettas, Shakedown
122	23 January 1982	The Greyhound, Chadwell Heath	Lambrettas, Fast Eddie
123	14 April 1982	The Venue, Victoria	Lambrettas, Jam Tarts

Appendix 2: Gig List 2009 to Date

	DATE	VENUE/LOCATION	APPEARING (Headliner first)
1	15 August 2009	Concorde2, Brighton	Lambrettas, Mark Joseph, The Hiwatts, Long Tall Shorty, Timebomb
2	15 November 2009	The 100 Club, London	Lambrettas, Teenbeats, Long Tall Shorty
3	11 December 2009	Finns, Weymouth	Lambrettas, The Lo Numbers
4	2 January 2010	The Soundbar, Birmingham	Lambrettas, The Upper Fifth, Rudie & the Revolvers, J60
5	5 February 2010	The Square, Harlow	Lambrettas, Long Tall Shorty
6	12 February 2010	Live@Dickens, Rotherham	Lambrettas, Sons of Elroacho
7	13 February 2010	Rios, Leeds	Lambrettas, Blackwater
8	19 February 2010	Whelans, Dublin	Lambrettas
9	26 February 2010	The Leopard, Doncaster	Lambrettas, The Black Ivories
10	27 February 2010	Basingstoke SC, The Academy Club, Basingstoke	Lambrettas
11	6 March 2010	12 Bar Club, Swindon	Lambrettas, Long Tall Shorty, The Suspicions
12	20 March 2010	The Crooked Billet, Essex	Lambrettas
13	28 March 2010	Moho, Manchester	Lambrettas, The Minx, Physical Jerks, The Ambush
14	4 April 2010	Mods for Heroes The Soundbar, Birmingham	Lambrettas, Glass Onion, Rudie & the Revolvers, J60, The Heels
15	10 April 2010	Joiners, Southampton	Lambrettas
16	7 May 2010	Hucknall SC, The Leisure Club Nottingham	Lambrettas
17	21 May 2010	The Beat Route, Congleton	Lambrettas, The Way, Eton Park
18	22 May 2010	The Brumby, Scunthorpe	Lambrettas, Fallen Zero
19	11 June 2010	The Old Bell, Derby	Lambrettas, The Roulettes
20	19 June 2010	Portsmouth Scooter Weekender, Moneyfields, Portsmouth	Lambrettas, The Racketeers
21	3 July 2010	Camber Sands Scooter Rally, Pontins Camber Sands	Lambrettas, Smodati, Squire Circle

22	28 August 2010	IOW Scooter Rally, The Ice Rink, Isle of Wight	Lambrettas, various bands
23	4 September 2010	Grumpy's Music Bar, Runcorn	Lambrettas, The Amnesiacs
24	9 September 2010	The Marrs Bar, Worcester	Lambrettas
25	10 September 2010	Dexters, Dundee	Lambrettas, Aka Ska
26	9 October 2010	Stanley Theatre, Liverpool	Lambrettas, Modern Works
27	3 December 2010	The Palace, Aldershot	From The Jam, Lambrettas
28	7 December 2010	Mr Kyps, Poole	Lambrettas, Austen Brown
29	8 December 2010	Robin 2, Wolverhampton	Lambrettas, The Uppers, The Sound
30	9 December 2010	The Clarendon, Hartlepool	Lambrettas, Modern Works
31	10 December 2010	The Club, Carlisle	Lambrettas
32	11 December 2010	Café Drummonds, Aberdeen	Lambrettas, The Targets
33	12 December 2010	Ivory Blacks, Glasgow	Lambrettas
34	14 December 2010	Moho, Manchester	Lambrettas, The Offenders
35	15 December 2010	The Well, Leeds	Lambrettas
36	16 December 2010	Live@Dickens, Rotherham	Lambrettas
37	17 December 2010	Underworld, Camden	Lambrettas, Mr Bridger
38	18 December 2010	The Brass Monkey, Hastings	Lambrettas, The Bleeding Hearts
39	19 March 2011	The Bitter End, Romford	Lambrettas, Mr Bridger
40	1 April 2011	The Forum, Waterford, Eire	Lambrettas, The Toniks
41	2 April 2011	The Village, Dublin, Eire	From The Jam, Lambrettas
42	25 June 2011	The Alley Club, The Haymakers, Cambridge	Lambrettas, Sta Prest, The Scene
43	15 July 2011	Guilfest, Vive Le Rock tent, Guildford	Various bands, Lambrettas, Various bands
44	23 July 2011	Lincoln Knights SC Sobraon Barracks, Lincoln	Lambrettas
45	17 September 2011	The Spring & Airbrake Belfast	Lambrettas, The Penny Dreadfuls, Monotonous Tones
46	23 September 2011	The Victoria Inn, Derby	Lambrettas, The Cedars
47	24 September 2011	Ribble Valley Mod Soul Wkender The Grand, Clitheroe	Lambrettas, DC Fontana, The Shades
48	30 September 2011	Hercules Hall, Portmeirion, North Wales	Lambrettas
49	22 October 2011	Cityfest, Guildford	Lambrettas, 9 other bands
50	26 November 2011	229 Club, London	Secret Affair, Lambrettas
51	5 December 2011	Purple Festival, Leon, Spain	Buzzcocks, Lambrettas, The Masonics
52	17 December 2011	Craflwynn Hall, Beddgelert, North Wales (Private wedding)	Lambrettas

53	30 December 2011	Torino, Italy	Lambrettas, Statuto
54	3 February 2012	The Globe, Cardiff	Lambrettas
55	4 February 2012	Sketchley Bar, Worcester	Lambrettas
56	24 March 2012	Clacton Weekender	Lambrettas, various
57	28 April 2012	Great British Alternative Festival, Minehead, (Centre Stage)	From The Jam, The Beat, Lambrettas
58	6 May 2012	Modrophenia 2012, 229, London	From The Jam, Lambrettas
59	20 July 2012	Joiners, Southampton	Lambrettas, The Butterfly Collective, England Road, The Uptights
60	22 September 2012	Looe Music Festival, Cornwall (Beach stage)	The Stranglers, The Levellers, Lambrettas, various bands – about 100
61	28 September 2012	Wurlitzer Ballroom, Madrid	Lambrettas
62	20 October 2012	Kings Hall, Stoke-on-Trent	Secret Affair, Lambrettas
63	23 November 2012	Concorde 2, Brighton	Secret Affair, Lambrettas
64	24 November 2012	229, London	Secret Affair, Lambrettas
65	01 December 2012	The Globe, Cardiff	Lambrettas, The Universal
66	02 February 2013	Shrewsbury Severnside Lions SC event, Lord Hill Hotel, Shrewsbury	Lambrettas, The Clocktower
67	09 February 2013	Band on the Wall, Manchester	Lambrettas, The Romleys
68	30 March 2013	Epic, Norwich	Secret Affair, Lambrettas
69	20 April 2013	The Kingfisher, Ipswich	Lambrettas, Million Faces
70	26 April 2013	Great British Alternative Festival, Minehead, (Reds Stage)	Eddie & the Hotrods, Lambrettas
71	01 June 2013	Billericay Football Club, Essex	Lambrettas, The Weller Collective
72	08 June 2013	100 Club, London	Lambrettas, Squire
73	22 June 2013	Peacehaven Music Festival	Lambrettas, various bands
74	28 June 2013	North Wales Scooter Rally, Bangor	Lambrettas, Jam DRC, various bands
75	29 June 2013	Stone Valley Scooter & Music Festival, Stanhope, Co. Durham	Lambrettas, Rudie & the Revolvers, The Universal, The Style Selektors
76	13 July 2013	Carnglaze Caverns, Cornwall	Lambrettas, James Robinson Band
77	27 July 2013	Scoot Arena, Kings Lynn	Lambrettas, Small Fakers, Scooted & Booted
78	10 August 2013	Jack up the 80s Festival, Isle of Wight	Bad Manners, Lambrettas, Dr & the Medics, Katrina & the Waves, Matchbox
79	11 August 2013	United Colours of Music Festival, Sheffield	Skatalites, Lee Thompson Ska Orchestra, Cockney Rejects, Lambrettas, Uplifters, Reasons To Be Cheerful, Benson

80	24 August 2013	Upton Music Festival, Worcester (Main stage)	Take Fat, Bad Manners, The Wurzels, Lambrettas, Neville Staple Band, Toyah Wilcox, Bucks Fizz, China Crisis
81	07 September 2013	A2aces Scooter Rally, Larne, Northern Ireland	Lambrettas, Doghouse
82	12 October 2013	Tonic 2 Festival, Portsmouth (Main stage)	The Dub Pistols with Terry Hall, From the Jam, Lambrettas, Parlour Flames, Orange Street, Small Fakers, Stefikie
83	19 October 2013	Skamouth Festival, Great Yarmouth	Neville Staple Band, Susan Cadogan, Lambrettas, The Dualers, The Downsetters
84	29 October 2013	Shocktoberfest, Tulleys Farm, Turners Hill	Lambrettas
85	02 November 2013	Concorde 2, Brighton	Secret Affair, Lambrettas
86	02 February 2014	80s weekend Butlins, Bognor	Bootleg Blondie, Lambrettas
87	28 February 2014	80s weekend Butlins, Minehead	Musical Youth, Lambrettas, Ex Simple Minds
88	22 March 2014	The Picturedrome, Northampton	Lambrettas, The Style Selektors, Ordinary Affair, The Remnants, Crossfire
89	19 April 2014	The Stags Head, Westbourne	Lambrettas
90	4 May 2014	Mods Mayday, Ida Darwin Club, Cambridge	Lambrettas, Chords UK, The Name
91	25 May 2014	Bournemouth Pier	Lambrettas, The Decatonics
92	28 June 2014	Queens Hall, Nuneaton	Lambrettas
93	06 September 2014	The Pig in Paradise, Hastings	Lambrettas
94	13 September 2014	The Custard House, Birmingham	Lambrettas, The Coopers, Samuel Rogers Band
95	19 September 2014	Looe Music Festival, Cornwall (Westons Cider stage Harbour Marquee)	Brand New Heavies, The Selector, Lambrettas, various bands (140 in total)
96	03 October 2014	Ultimate 80's , Butlins, Skegness (Reds Stage)	Alexander O'Neal, Lambrettas, Ex Simple Minds, various bands
97	12 October 2014	GBAF, Butlins, Skegness (Reds Stage)	From The Jam, Lambrettas, various bands
98	24 October 2014	The Dome, Liverpool	Secret Affair, Lambrettas, The Universal
99	08 November 2014	The City Hall, Salisbury	Secret Affair, Lambrettas

100	21 November 2014	The Drill Hall, Lincoln	Secret Affair, Lambrettas
101	22 November 2014	The Britannia, Dickens World, Chatham	Secret Affair, Lambrettas
102	29 November 2014	Under The Bridge, London	Secret Affair, Lambrettas
103	06 February 2015	MkII Live Music Venue, Milton Keynes	Lambrettas, + 2 support bands
104	07 February 2015	The Box, Crewe	Lambrettas, Skaface
105	28 February 2015	The Froddington Arms, Portsmouth	Lambrettas, The Novatones
106	14 March 2015	Ropetackle Arts Centre, Shoreham	Lambrettas
107	17 April 2015	Hertford Corn Exchange, Hertford	Lambrettas, Quixotes Beard
108	23 April 2015	The Guildhall, Preston	Secret Affair, Lambrettas
109	8 May 2015	The Haunt, Brighton	Lambrettas, The Novatones, Infersound
110	9 May 2015	100 Club, London	Lambrettas, The Novatones
111	23 May 2015	The Doghouse, Nottingham	Lambrettas, Gentleman Rogues, Garden Gang
112	24 May 2015	Riverside Festival, Co. Durham	FTJ, The Selector, Secret Affair, Lambrettas, various others
113	30 May 2015	The Junction, Cambridge	Lambrettas, The Circles
114	12 June 2015	The Riverfront, Newport	Lambrettas, Junior Hacksaw, Keep it in the Dark
115	19 June 2015	The Corporation Club, Hartlepool	Lambrettas, Dig the Old Breed, The Little Details
116	20 June 2015	Davey's Sports & Social Centre, Sheffield	Beat Goes Bang, Lambrettas, various others
117	11 July 2015	Lewes Live Festival	Lambrettas, various 12 other bands
118	31 July 2015	The Music Room, Ipswich	Lambrettas, Ska'd for Life
119	30 August 2015	Great Northern Mod & Ska Festival, Bedale, North Yorkshire Main Stage)	Bad Manners, Lambrettas, Chords UK, various others
120	26 September 2015	Valencia Scooter Club, Valencia, Spain	Lambrettas, The Bell Boys
121	16 October 2015	The Beachcomber, Cleethorpes	Secret Affair, Lambrettas
122	17 October 2015	Haig Mining & Colliery Museum, Whitehaven, Cumbria	Lambrettas, Acoustic Support
123	23 October 2015	The Globe, Cardiff	Lambrettas, The Riff
124	14 November 2015	The Ambience Club, Pontefract	Lambrettas, Jonny Boy Pryor
125	3 December 2015	The Brook, Southampton	Secret Affair, Chords UK, Lambrettas
126	26 March 2016	Select Security Stadium, Widnes	Lambrettas, The Jam DRC, Deadbeat Decendants, Indigo Violet

127	27 March 2016	Bristol Ska & Mod Festival, Bristol (Main Stage)	From The Jam, The Beat, Lambrettas, Dub Pistols, 2Rude & Roddy Radiation, The Small Fakers
128	23 April 2016	Sabinillas Scooter Festival, Costa del Sol, Spain	Lambrettas, Mentally Ska'd
129	6 May 2016	100 Club, London	Lambrettas, Chords UK, Squire
130	7 May 2016	The Empress Suite, Worthing	Lambrettas, The Gangsters
131	21 May 2016	Löwenberger Land, near Berlin, Germany, (Private wedding)	Lambrettas, 2 other bands
132	28 May 2016	Snowdonia Scooter Rally, Porthmadog, North Wales	Lambrettas, The Insiders
133	18 August 2016	The Trades, Rotherham	Lambrettas, Hospital Food
134	19 August 2016	The Bellfield Tavern, Kilmarnock, Scotland	Lambrettas, Mod Life Crisis, Dogtooth
135	20 August 2016	Penicuik Town Hall, Penicuik, Scotland	Lambrettas, The Redstarts
136	09 September 2016	Monkeys Music Club, Hamburg, Germany	Secret Affair, Lambrettas
137	06 October 2016	The Arc, Stockton	Lambrettas
138	07 October 2016	GBAF, Reds Stage, Butlins, Skegness	Anti Nowhere League, U.K. Subs, Lambrettas
139	02 December 2016	229 Club, London	Secret Affair, Lambrettas, Jel
140	09 December 2016	The Spring, Havant, Portsmouth	Lambrettas
141	04 February 2017	Bognorphenia, Riverside Caravan Centre, Bognor	Lambrettas
	10 March 2017	BBC Radio Cornwall Live Session, Truro, Cornwall	Not a gig, but live interview with David White and 2 live acoustic songs
142	11 March 2017	Skamodpunksoulfest, Tencreek Holiday Park, Looe, Cornwall	Lambrettas, The Kingstons, The Bubble
143	08 April 2017	Acapela, Pentrych, Nr Cardiff	Lambrettas
144	21 April 2017	Skamouth Festival, Great Yarmouth	Various bands, Lambrettas, various bands
145	05 May 2017	100 Club, London	Lambrettas, Chords UK, Squire
146	20 May 2017	Lambretta Club Lomardia SR, F1 Circuit, Monza, Italy	Lambrettas, The Mads
147	27 May 2017	Lechlade Festival, Cotswolds, Gloucestershire	The Hoosiers, Dr Feelgood, Lambrettas, various bands (100 in total)
148	24 June 2017	Modfest on Beach, Grand Pavilion, Porthcawl, Wales	Secret Affair, Lambrettas, Special Brew

149	08 July 2017	Cleethorpes SR, Waves Bar, Cleethorpes	Lambrettas, All Mod Cons
150	15 July 2017	Modfest on Beach, Morecambe Winter Gardens, Morecambe	Secret Affair, Lambrettas, Mancheter Ska Foundation, Deep Six
151	06 August 2017	Music Mania Festival, Worthing Rugby Club	Lambrettas, Chords UK, Signatures, Butterfly Collective, Blurb, Urang Matang
152	12 August 2017	Dunoon Revival weekender, Scotland	Lambrettas, Resurrection Stone Roses, The 45's, P.O.O., Seaside Sons, The Redstarts, Cherry Red 53
153	30 September 2017	Exeter Phoenix, Exeter	Lambrettas, Chords UK
154	24 November 2017	Clapham Grand, London	From The Jam, Lambrettas
155	04 May 2018	229 Club, London	Secret Affair. Lambrettas, Chords UK, Squire, various other bands
156	30 June 2018	Stone Valley Festival, (North), Stanhope, Co. Durham	Stiff Little Fingers, From The Jam, Lambrettas, various other bands
157	14 July 2018	The Coal Exchange, Cardiff	Lambrettas, Chords UK, The Navarones, The Underclass, The Future Sailors
158	06 October 2018	Waterloo Music Bar, Blackpool	Lambrettas, The Immediates, Small Weller, Dogtooth
159	07 October 2018	GBAF, Reds Stage, Butlins, Skegness	Angelic Upstarts, The Professionals, Lambrettas
160	19 October 2018	Downham Market Town Hall	Lambrettas, Chords UK
161	03 November 2018	Cutlers Arms, Rotherham	Lambrettas, Handsome Dan & The Mavericks, The Time Sellers
162	23 November 2018	Skamouth Festival, Great Yarmouth	Various bands, Lambrettas, various bands
163	09 March 2019	GBAF, Reds Stage, Butlins, Minehead	The Jam Restart, Toyah, Lambrettas
164	05 May 2019	Islington Assembly Hall, London	Secret Affair, The Truth, The Lambrettas, The Vapors, Circles, Squire, Chords UK
165	27 May 2019	Darwen Live Festival, Darwen, Lancs	Toyah, The Lambrettas, Electrik Dreams, Skapones, 5th Element, Sound of the Sirens, Gemma Louise Doyle

Lambrettas Discography

Year	Title	Label	Track Listing		
1980	Beat Boys in the Jet Age	Rocket Records			
1981	Ambience	Rocket Records			
1985	Kick Start (compliation)				
	The Singles				
1979	Go Steady	Rocket Records	!	Go Steady	
			!	Cortina	
			!	Listen Listen	
1980	Poison Ivy	Rocket Records	!	Poison Ivy	
			!	Runaround	
1980	D-a-a-ance	Rocket Records	!	D-a-a-ance	
			!	Can't You Feel The Beat	
1980	Another Day (Another Girl)	Rocket Records	!	Another Day (Another Girl)	
			!	Steppin' Out Of Line	
1981	Good Times	Rocket Records	!	Good Times	
			!	Lamba Samba	
1981	Anything You Want	Rocket Records	!	Anything You Want	
			!	Ambience	
1981	Decent Town	Rocket Records	!	Decent Town	
			!	D-a-a-ance (Live in Europe)	
1981	Decent Town 12" version	Rocket Records	!	Decent Town	
			!	Total Strangers	
			!	D-a-a-ance (Live in Europe)	
			!	Young Girls (Live in Europe)	
1982	Somebody To Love	Rocket Records	!	Somebody To Love	
			!	Nobody's Watching Me	

The Compact Discs		
1994	Beat Boys in the Jet Age	Dojo
1995	Best of The Lambrettas The Singles Collection	Dojo
1996	Ambience	Dojo
1998	The Definitive Collection Beat Boys in The Jet Age 2 x CD Compilation	Castle Communications
2000	The Definitive Collection Beat Boys in The Jet Age 2 x CD Compilation	Sanctuary Records
2002	D-a-a-ance (The Lambrettas Anthology) 2 x CD Compilation	Castle Music
2015	Beat Boys in The Jet Age 2 x CD Compilation	Salvo
2017	Go 4 It 4 x Track EP	Jet Age Records
Vinyl EP		
2017	Go 4 It 5 x Track EP	Jet Age Records